BFI Modern Classics

D0489577

Rob White
Series Editor

BFI Modern Classics is a series of critical studies of films produced over the last three decades. An array of writers explore their chosen films, offering a range of perspectives on the dominant art and entertainment medium in contemporary culture. The series gathers together snapshots of our passion for and understanding of recent movies.

Also Published

Eyes Wide Shut
Michel Chion

Heat
Nick James
(see a full list of titles in the series at the back of this book)

Forthcoming

City of Sadness
Berenice Reynaud

Dilwale Dulhaniya Le Jeyenge
Anupama Chopra

The Idiots
John Rockwell

LA Confidential
Manohla Dargis

Jaws

Antonia Quirke

 Publishing

For Eric Gordon, editor of the *Camden New Journal*.
And James.

First published in 2002 by the
British Film Institute
21 Stephen Street, London W1T 1LN

Copyright ©Antonia Quirke 2002

The British Film Institute promotes greater
understanding and appreciation of,
and access to, film and moving image
culture in the UK.

British Library Cataloguing-in-Publication Data
A catalogue record for this book is available
from the British Library

ISBN 0-85170-929-X

Series design by Andrew Barron &
Collis Clements Associates

Typeset in Italian Garamond and Swiss 721BT
by D R Bungay Associates, Burghfield, Berks

Printed in Great Britain by
Cromwell Press, Trowbridge, Wiltshire

Contents

Introduction *6*

The Land *9*

The Sea *58*

Credits *92*

Note on Sources *94*

Introduction

The shark was always a star. In July 1916, a Great White killed four bathers off the New Jersey shore and drove the Great War from the front pages of newspapers all over the world. The incidents became an instant myth, the fish instantly famous. Yet unlike other man-eating creatures, other notorious lions and leopards, it was unanthropomorphisable. It gathered no nicknames, no individual identity. And since no-one could be certain that the shark which was caught and held responsible really was the killer, it retained a certain bogeyman quality. Unexorcised, it diffused into the collective unconscious, reappearing fifty-seven years later in Peter Benchley's thriller *Jaws*, which was of no particular merit, even as a time-passing page-turner, but a spectacular success. Here was one of those stories which seems always to have been nebulously there, unformed but already comprehended, waiting for someone to come along and fix it, nail it, get it down right. And this is the first thing to say about the film of *Jaws*, which has this property of seeming discovered rather than created. It is definitive. It is the definitive articulation of a myth. It hits the nail right on the head.

That's the Spielberg touch. The direct hit which renders the film-maker's personality less visible than would a glancing blow. Given material too complex for a direct emotional bullseye – World War II, for instance, in California, China, Normandy or Central Europe – given a subject rather than a sensation, then he becomes both more legible and less himself. Not having an angle is his angle. Being effective is the sum of Spielberg's artistic vision – which made him for a long time extraordinarily difficult to categorise. His failures are not failures in an interesting way: they are simply less effective films. So picture him in 1974, one evening during the *Jaws* shoot, describing to Richard Dreyfuss all the possible angles he could push the film towards. Hitchcockian, Bergmanesque, Kubrickian, Altmanesque, Coppola-esque. Cormanesque. There's the Melville-thing. *The Enemy of the People* Ibsen–Watergate thing. The Vietnam-thing. This is the 1970s! There are subjects to respond to. And meanwhile, seemingly everywhere, his peers are all finding their own distinctive voices or visions: Bogdanovich, Scorsese, Friedkin, Coppola,

Malick, Lucas, all carving out niches. Whereas his first feature, *The Sugarland Express* (a film consistently overrated as underrated) has just failed commercially because, it appears, of its downbeat ending. Is he going to be painted into a shark-and-truck corner because of the perfect but limited *Duel*? Three times he's tried to get off this monster movie, has pleaded to be allowed something more serious, something which might be Spielbergian. He is twenty-seven, claims he's twenty-six and, naturally, he wants to be an artist, like Orson Welles. And *Jaws* has one *raison d'être* – to be a financial success.

But although he is under extraordinary pressure (and the pressure really is head-swimmingly intense and unrelenting) simply to get the film made at all, he is in a more important sense freer than he ever has been or will be again. This is an *assignment*, so he doesn't have to square it with his artistic conscience. It isn't *his* baby. And everyone knows it's an assignment so he doesn't have to be judged by it. The film belongs to a mixture of low genres so he doesn't have to invent tones, only orchestrate them, and he has plenty to play with. He has nothing, particularly, to communicate (and striving too hard to communicate emotion is what has vitiated Spielberg's whole career: it's what blights *Close Encounters*, *E.T.* and *Schindler's List*, his three favourite films). His actors are making up their lines which will never happen again. He has no reputation to live up to, no voice he need find. And vitally, his sense of humour has bumped into its perfect vehicle – a latent comedy. All he has to do is be effective. To nail that shark.

Which, famously, was not easy. I'm not going to detail the nightmarish production in this book since screenwriter Carl Gottlieb's classic diary *The Jaws Log* is an unimprovable record of the shoot – and an unsurpassed description of collaboration in film-making. But it's worth noting, with regard to the collaborative nature of *Jaws*, that Spielberg was the driving force behind these four decisions: no stars, real sea, likeable characters instead of the Benchley sourpusses, and a mainly implied shark. (Neither will I detail what happened next, this particularly melancholy history of a *succés fou* and its whole new species of phenomenon-money – the very money that supposedly ruined everything and led to the wasteland of the 1980s. It's a story Peter Biskind has told.)

Scarred by the experience of the shoot, Spielberg was never particularly fond of his smash hit. 'I look back at that film', he once said, 'and it seems like it was a different person making it.' It was. Gone now that freewheeling, youth-dependent deadpan–sarcastic sense of humour. Probably Spielberg knows that *Jaws'* brand of sly comedy cannot be planned, and he has never attempted anything like it again. He has made films which are more personal to him, but never anything more personal to his talent – and it's Spielberg's talent, not his taste, which we can trust. *Jaws* is his nimblest, crispest and best film, and being so light and foxy, still underrated. It's a minor classic. Or, as we tend to put it, a modern classic.

The Land

**THIRD FISHERMAN: Master, I marvel how the fishes live in the sea.
FIRST FISHERMAN: Why, as men do a-land; the great ones eat up the
little ones.**

William Shakespeare, *Pericles*

1. Shame

Before you know it, before you expect it, there's a sound. The screen is
dark, giving us time to settle down, that private second before it all begins.
But there's a sound, and we have to listen.

It's the sound of marine life. A whale, perhaps? Dolphins. Sonar. At
first it seems to reflect us. Sea-babble to accompany audience-babble, the
sea version of the chatter of the cinema audience finding seats and taking
off coats and finishing arguments and keeping an eye out for latecomers.
But really it's the sound of a sea orchestra tuning up, waiting for the
soloist. The shark.

As soon as he starts playing, the blather is silenced, on screen and
off. He moves through the water – this tuba, this double bass, this far end
of the piano – with a roving eye. He's at the bottom of the sea, brushing
through kelp forests, like a convict escaping through some strange field.
John Williams' theme is at once serious and comical, solemn and skittish,
building until it's almost a refrain from *West Side Story* – that scene at the
dance when the Jets and the Sharks circle each other with crouching
daring, sure that everything to come is going to be heroic and mutinous
and fun. But it's over very quickly.

The break of rhythm in the credits is so unusual, a jump-cut,
and the next wail we hear comes very much from the land, from a
harmonica played badly round a beach fire. It is night. Someone else is
playing the guitar. You know this group of people are not really hippies –
they're smoking cigarettes rather than roll-ups, and there's something
about their hair that suggests it can be made to look neat for the country
club.

Any one of these kids could be Steven Spielberg. Before he made *Jaws*, he'd sit on the beach in LA watching Brian De Palma and Paul Schrader and the rest of that gang as they felt up each other's girlfriends, did a line, got in a mess. He knew it wasn't for him, that he wasn't *curious* like that. And he was suspicious of the kind of person who pretended to be.

Eight years earlier Spielberg had made a card-calling short *Amblin'* which was all about a guy who chased a free-spirited girl across southern California en route to the Pacific coast. Just a preppy slumming it for a week or two, a poser with mouth wash and loo roll secreted in his backpack. The blonde man that the camera now finds on the *Jaws* beach, sloshed in a mumsy jumper, is rather like that character. He's sitting with his back against the fire looking at the blonde girl in the shadows near the fence.

She seems to be the real thing, her eyes properly bright. She's clearly not one of this gang, this summer seascape family. She's not sheltering by the cosy fire, not swigging from a can. She keeps her little tasselled bag at her feet like someone used to making a quick getaway, someone who leaves nothing behind. The two blondes run down to the sea. Her voice is childish. She says her name. Chrissie. He's having trouble taking off his clothes (good cords, a good shirt) but she's naked in seconds (clothes? disposable!) and in the water. You wonder if Chrissie is a conventional siren, luring this mummy's boy to a watery death, but what's the worry? You don't care for him much.

The drunk and predatory preppy

Suddenly, our anxiety switches on. Chrissie is shown at a distance, making her leg disappear into the water like a gentle periscope. It's so Bond girl. As are the first shots of her from beneath – a mermaid gliding and tumbling to a new Williams theme, a harp in ecstasy, tumescent and hallucinatory.

Back on the beach mummy's boy collapses saying: 'I can swim. Just can't walk, or dress myself.' He might be speaking for the shark, who now watches this girl as she floats, bright against the moonlight. But it could be day. She's a sun-ray to the eyes of one who spends his life hidden in a one-windowed pit. His is an ancient gaze of longing and envy. He wants her and her medium. He wants to break out of his psychopathic haze and capture the world of health and air and brown limbs and thick golden hair. If she were wearing a skirt he'd look up it now, because he's powerless, a dirty little beast, a Humbert Humbert who fears this particular Dolores might 'explode in screams if I touched her with any part of my wretchedness'.

As the shark moves in on Chrissie it's almost as though he's stepping in, knowing she's been let down by a lover, tapping on her foot, trying to be gallant. But she won't go down to him willingly. You notice her earrings. Silver hoops. They surprise you, remind you that she is human. Not a siren come from a coral cave to bewitch a sailor. Not a mermaid who belongs to the sea. She's a bold girl wearing nothing but a pair of silver hoops, looking mildly humorous and intent, waiting for some college kid to finally get his kit off, brave the waves, and kiss her.

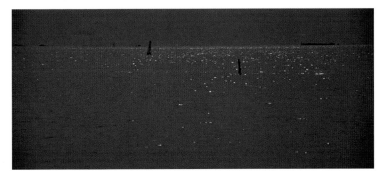

Chrissie as siren

That's why her death is unconventionally protracted, longer than your average screen murder.

Chrissie turns her secret suitor down and suffers something as long as a screen rape. You wonder if the shark is under the impression she's enjoying it, because he takes his time, takes her for a ride. Literally. She is swept along to the right and then to the left, the graceful curve of her wet shoulders the only thing that's visible. For a second she turns her head to look down, like someone hoping to emerge out of the sea on someone's shoulders, having taken part in nothing more than a cruel play-fight.

The shark even gives her (and us) a moment's break, a mini interval, allowing Chrissie to hold on to a buoy, to catch her breath, to shiver. We

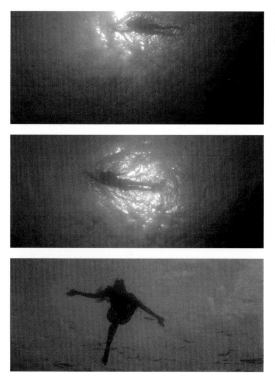

The shark gazes longingly at this mermaid or angel

The rape: as in *Psycho*'s shower scene, the violence is both implied and overwhelming

know that she's praying and sobbing, but the shark doesn't. He isn't listening. He can't perceive what happens above the surface. Chrissie's death is the perfect metaphor for casual sex – a communication breakdown between above and below, mental and physical.

When she's gone the music stops, and there's nothing but the sound of the sea and the buoy, which doesn't so much give our guts time to settle down, as leave us incontrovertibly aware of the mute act of witnessing.

What's next? Where to now? Should we giggle? The still-dressed blonde guy lies prone in the surf. He burps.

2. Denial

It's the exposure Martin Brody can't get used to. In New York he couldn't sleep for the weight. But here it's just miles of air and he can't shake this feeling of being opened. Look at the Atlantic! His house is full of it. And all this demanding light come to wake him! How come the sun never used to shine out here?

'Because we bought the house in the fall,' says his wife. 'Now it's summer.' Ellen tastes her own early-morning metallic breath. She watches her husband get slowly out of bed. His shorts are too big at the back, hinting that weariness has withered his bottom. Their dog sits in the bed like marriage, glancing at the camera until it remembers Mr Spielberg told it not to. There was a time when Michael and Sean jumped in and forced Ellen and Martin up at six, but since the family moved to Amity Island the kids are straight out of the house in the mornings. That's something you don't get in the city, the kids playing in the innocent yard. 'In Amity,' teases Ellen, 'you say yaad.'

'They're in the yaad not too faar from the caar,' manages Brody with elongated Boston vowels. 'How's that?'

'Like you're from New York,' says Ellen.

Which Brody doesn't like to remember. It's so easy to imagine this man returning home every night from the streets of Brooklyn, feeling the city like an ache under the skin, needing to be comforted by his wife. But Chief of Police in Amity is about as far from the front line as you can get. When the station calls him with news of a girl possibly drowned, it's the most excitement there's been for a month.

Roy Scheider and his amazing skin

The film's crisp, toy-bright, painterly look

   Here's Brody in the kitchen on the phone, so neat. Spielberg shoves the camera right up to Roy Scheider's face, a thirty-nine year-old New York actor who wanted to be in *Jaws* because he met Spielberg at a Christmas party and liked the sound of this more-than-a-sidekick cop, a character slightly more median than his star turn in *The French Connection*. And like all actors, he needed the work. The whole notion of actors making choices is a journalistic distortion: very few of them are prom queens holding out for the best-looking date, and even those prom queens are at the mercy of random accident. We notice, as we always do with Scheider, his perfect parting. His antelope eyes. His skin tanned and creased like a loved handbag. And Ellen over his shoulder as he hangs up rinsing her eldest son's cut hand under the tap. Blood and water.

   When Brody leaves he's holding his wife's mug and is sashed with her prim tea-towel. Outside it's wildly bright and the house looks shocking. It's a toy house, a holiday home, coy with its powder-blue shutters. Surely adults can't really live here, rounded every day by sand? But Ellen wanted it on first sight. New Yorkers too smart to go to Coney Island or the Jersey shore come to Amity for their holidays, and she adored the island's clapboard clarity, its promise of eternal breeze. And so the family migrated from the urban breeding grounds. They're on permanent vacation. Like that Amazonian beach babe on the billboard near the house, Amity's Statue of Liberty, laughing in her bikini season round.

   Like I'm from New York thinks the man who didn't stay and fight, the man who rejected the present tense, the one thing worth fighting for. The act of down-shifting, the Peter Mayle dream, is almost always a cover-up. You can't, with physical well-being and nursery paint, mask everything you've known, everything you've seen. Because the act of retreat is a regression through time. You will never belong. And if you run to the past you're using up civilisation instead of adding to it. Which is something Ellen and Martin don't talk about. It's the silence in their marriage, emerging in tiny accidental needlings. But isn't this preferable to New York? The air is pure, the traffic non-existent, and here he is in his pride-

and-joy jeep going to work on a beach! Not even the kid from last night can put him off his stride.

In the daylight he looks ironed, this kid. Richer, more spoilt and seemingly more concerned above all to conceal the damage to his sexual pride. 'No sir! She didn't run out on me!' He's no longer a resident of the island notes Brody as they proceed along the shoreline, and yet still retains that unpierceable them-and-us parochialism he and Ellen keep bumping up against. Oh! There's a blast on the whistle from Brody's deputy, and everything starts to go wrong.

No-one can look at what's left of Chrissie. Neither the kid, nor the camera, which shows us only the crabs crawling over her nails – sharp objects to needle our nerves. The deputy has fallen to the sand, his mouth

The deputy's averted face

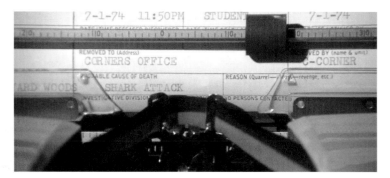

Brody doesn't mince his words

wet with panic, his face averted, like James Dean agonising on the pavement in *East of Eden*. It's such a self-consciously old-fashioned moment that it can't fail to further identify Chrissie as a victim of rape. But Brody looks, and then he turns, his soft parting ruffled, to look at the sea. His main suspect.

Probable cause of death, Brody types back at base, is 'SHARK ATTACK'. What's this? A detective story in which the cop's first guess is right! Unheard of. Not only does this make one doubt in the shark, it simultaneously avoids any tedious Hollywood vacillations – you know, all those films that start with the 'will the cop come out of retirement to take on a last case' set-up that have you muttering *Oh, for God's sake, get a move on!* So you *know* it's a shark but it will *feel* for a long time like a bluff.

But to Brody it's very refreshing, the kind of clear and purposeful police-work you never get in New York. The right course of action is simple. And how delightful, really, to be up of a morning closing the beaches, as he intends to do. The birds sing and win a little smile from him. The cherry-blossom wins a little skip. The freshness of the air wins a little sniff. And Spielberg, taking us on a tour around the Disney set of Amity town is openly giggling, reassuring us that he's too young and too droll to make a film about small-town narrowness. He showers us with picket fences, mocking the cliché by overwhelming us with it. Look, a joke! Brody, in a hurry, dutifully follows the right-angle of the pedestrian crossing rather than cutting a corner. Listen! The Amity High School Band rehearsing for the Fourth of July drum out the cop's raised heartbeat. This wholly unexpected daisy-fresh tone!

Cut into this are the Amity newspaper editor, coroner and mayor, who have been apprised on the Amity bush telegraph of Brody's intentions. And how do we know that this mayor, Larry Vaughn, is a sod? He jaywalks. These three catch Martin on the car ferry that shuttles between the two points of Amity bay – he intends to warn some swimmers of their danger – and quench him and the film of motion. Naturally, Amity being 'a summer town which needs summer dollars', a cover-up is being instigated. 'If people can't swim here they'll swim at Cape Cod!' Brody is outnumbered. All his constriction and bewilderment is expressed by a long, long take on a static camera which swings with the ferry through a 180-degree portrait of the island. Suffocating and dizzying. Larry holds a pretend cigarette and exudes the sweated scent of effort. He talks in a purely musical impersonation of speech, like a seedy compère coaxing the audience to 'Call me Larry'.

It's a summer town and the biggest day in the calendar looms. Chrissie died in a boating accident and there is no shark. In doubting this for even for a second Martin has proved one thing. He is from New York.

Amity as a Disney set

Beautifully blocked – Brody squeezed against the edge of the frame

3. Dread

What's it like to be a fat actor? The kind of jobbing pro ever cast as clownish or gauche or misanthropic. What's it like to be a fat extra? Simply there to project 'I like fish paste and porridge and will never be bronzed and buoyant and slim-hipped'. There's a huge woman in a demure green and white bathing suit crossing the beach now. Her presence refers back to a moment before, when Brody pointed out to Larry that keeping the beaches open would be like serving the shark smorgasbord. It's a funny line. And then the smorgasbord enters the surf.

How did Spielberg phrase why he'd picked her? Did she enjoy her afternoon's work, this woman, cast to look like the main course to Chrissie's starter? She's an important figure, challenging to us to imagine the shark as simply practical, not a *lech*. Charles Bruder, a bell-captain half-eaten by a Great White in the same waters some sixty years before muttered before he died: 'He's a big fellow, and awfully hungry.' The kind of shark who'd go for smorgasbord?

Girls in swimsuits have always had the violence they enact on the male eye dreamed back on them by men. Bikini, you may remember, is

Pablo Picasso, *Ball Players on the Beach* (August 1928) © Succession Picasso / DACS 2002

the name of the atoll where the first postwar atomic test was made. Boom being the whole idea. Did you know they used to think near-naked women attracted sharks? On the beaches off the southern coast of New Jersey just before World War I young people made eyes and wore daring costumes. Legs were shown. In 1916 the *Philadelphia Evening Bulletin* ran the headline 'Startling Hosiery Fad Rules The Beach' noting that ladies were showing their knees. Frowns were made, sometimes arrests, with tape-measures. 'It draws too many sharks,' complained the lifeguards.

But the legs kept coming. A decade later Scott Fitzgerald and his gang had invented the Riviera, heading to the Hotel du Cap, swimming 'choppy little four beat crawls' out to rafts and pulling each other gently out of the heat and allowing it to seep into the corners of their bodies. 'I say. They have sharks out behind the raft,' thrills Campion in *Tender is the Night*. 'Yesterday they devoured two British sailors from the flotte at Golfe-Juan.' 'Heavens!' exclaims the pretty heroine. Coco Chanel also caught the sun that year, and Man Ray was in Biarritz making a short film about the beach that was nothing *but* legs. Long freckled legs in the sand, legs fidgeting with emancipation. And soon all these legs, these women, their boyfriends, their husbands and their children came to love the beach. They wore less and less. Thighs were seen. Alcohol was brought in coolers. Cream to ensure even more hours could be spent there – dawn till dusk. What did we do with our success as a species except yearn to fritter our time, to feel sun-baked and superfluous, lacking in purpose for two weeks every summer? Ever since, society's been trying to rehabilitate leisure as something important to productivity. We are, apparently, more efficient when rested. But doesn't excess leisure just aggravate the pressure human beings feel to justify their life? To have a point.

It's dreamy down by the seaside. A place to be supine. The way Spielberg shoots this beach is perfectly drowsy. He holds back with his close-ups (an economy he claimed to have learned from John Ford) allowing the frieze of people and all the segments and curves of primary colours to fill the screen, like Seurat's famous image of the Seine or Picasso's beach paintings. The camera imitates a sunbather's lazy eye, tracking all this happy flesh. It's

All the possible victims (the dog via its stick) are linked by the idea of floating – the surface of the water is the focus of anxiety

rather like watching tropical fish. You choose and follow your favourite hedonist among these toddlers, these parents, these lovers. The beach spells human variety at its most visible, and for the next few minutes of the film we too are suspended in an unhurried afternoon tending nowhere, with rubbish on the radio. Time off.

And the dark thread of purpose woven through this scene – dread of the shark – is also the linear motion of time which beach life, with its rejuvenating daydreams, its childishness, its sandload of truants, its undemanding beach-reads (that trashy new bestseller about a killer shark, for instance) tries to deny.

'What I want to know,' Ellen enquires of a friend, a brash blasé Amityite of about her own age, 'is when do I get to become an islander?'

'Ellen, never. Never! You're not born here, that's it!'

Since, as ever, there's nothing urgently requiring Brody's attention at the office he's accompanied Ellen and the kids to the beach. Perhaps Larry is right. A boating accident, a propeller slicing through a swimmer

The poster for the Royal Academy's *Apocalypse* show, design by Why Not Associates

would be a mess. Nonetheless he feels compelled to be here, watching over his flock. Like us, Brody is armed with nothing more than a gaze. The camera is simultaneously leaning intently forward (Brody's paranoid POV) and slouched back in its deckchair (the indolently roving beach eye) with brilliant yellow flash-frames of people passing by, obscuring our view. We find ourselves trying, with Brody, to crane round them as if we were trying to peer over the shoulder of summer itself. To peek at some horror. Look at the poster for the Royal Academy's *Apocalypse* exhibition. See how remarkable a cliché the hidden life of beaches has become! Any image of life and leisure presented without comment has come, sarcastically, to signify its exact opposite. But at the time of *Jaws* it was a fresh intuition.

To Brody's eye each image of bright playfulness conceals a vision of death. He's Dick Diver surveying his beach at Juans les Pins, seeing the awful underside of his kingdom. Brody spots smorgasbord flat on her back, floating, an estranged liferaft. The black bump now bearing down on her is only an outmoded swimming cap on the skull of the most benign-looking old man. Calm down, Brody! He allows a self-depreciating sweat to form on his forehead. And that girl, she's only screaming because her boyfriend's hoisting her out of the waves on his shoulders (great thighs). Don't cry wolf, Martin! This interweaving of false red herrings, real red herrings, bluffs and double bluffs does to us what it is doing to Brody. It tires us out. It's too much, this vigilance. And so Brody allows his son into the water with a slew of schoolmates, whooping and splashing. 'Chief Brody, you are uptight!' tuts Ellen, massaging his shoulders. Lucky him.

What do monsters prey on if not the unwary? Sometimes it seems we keep characters in films alive by riveting our attention on them, and so once our gaze has relaxed along with Brody's the editing rhythm collapses into cross-cutting and slopping water and blind self-absorbed noisiness as if to say *Now you've gone and done it. Now it's all going to pot.* And only now, when some measure of blame can be transferred to the no longer alert spectator, can the worst happen. We go under. Down, through the meniscus. This is *Jaws*' defining image – the shark's-eye division of the world into above and below. In order to take anyone the shark has to come to the surface, to risk breaking through and catch a glimpse of sandflies and bright shorts, a glimpse of what John Updike called 'the Dionysian potential of American life'. The text, the visible world, laughing heads. Below, the subtext. Everything that is withheld from the visible. Silence and headless bodies. Here is the full flowering of the particularly American paranoia that the apparent world is a façade laid over reality, which in time *The Truman Show* and *Capricorn One* and *The Matrix* would literalise with less delicacy and less horror.

Perhaps the shark chooses twelve year-old Alex Kintner because, floating horizontally on his lilo, he reminds him of Chrissie in her mermaid pose. There really is an atmosphere of *seeking* as, down where it's darkest blue, the shark hunts past limbs and limbs, rejecting one tender little leg in favour of this whole person further off. His lost love? It's a horrible attack. Not just because from the beach it looks like some heavy industrial machine (a mill-wheel of some kind) has destroyed something, but more because there's the lingering suspicion that the shark's motives are sexual and he's made a mistake. Alex is taken very quickly. Unenjoyed. Pulled low like someone falling down an elevator shaft. Both attacks are filmed *through* the moments of contact. For Chrissie the music never attained its climax by the time she was bitten, and Alex's end is filmed with an almost unruffled rhythm. This gives the attacks such reality. You are not allowed to think *Ah, the worst is over. The knife is in*. The moment of catharsis

Brody cannot go in

doesn't really come, and so the horror is never diffused, it's regretful and transfixed. Trustworthy.

Now Spielberg zooms the lens in whilst moving the camera backwards, to create the sensation of plunging from a castle parapet in the viewer – Hitchcock's trick in *Vertigo* which had them puking in the aisles. It shows us Brody, impotent in his deckchair, whizzing through stress, through a breathless five seconds of beholding. How old he looks! The crags and puddles of his face are very defined. His hair looks fluffy and benign. A man sketched in pencil. And now this pencil-man has to jump up and rush across the sand, directing others to pull the swimmers out of the sea. Brody is frightened of the water, and always has been. To him it's just a huge and unknowable surface, not really an element at all. And so he daren't plunge through, not even to save his own son. The shame of his having to watch Ellen rescue Michael is what makes the last few moments of the scene so plaintive. That and the other hunt happening now. Mother for child.

Just as Alex was the most desirable thing in the water to the shark, he is the most valuable thing on the beach. To Mrs Kintner. *No-one* could be more necessary to somebody else, not Michael to Ellen, Ellen to Brody. Instinctively we know that this woman is on her own. Earlier in the scene, when Alex asked for permission to go out for another few minutes, there was something about the way she wasn't luxuriating in the heat, but cradling a book in her peeved, white arms. Even though she wears a wedding ring, she is surely a widow. Not the kind of woman who suggests divorce. She held her son's fingers sensibly, complaining that they were pruning. She seemed a little overstrict, grasping those fingers, momentarily forgetful of how adorable they were.

The seconds of calm that follow everyone getting out of the water and clutching their companions is curtailed by the sight of Alex's chomped yellow lilo in the shallows. Its underside is black. How drenched we feel in the sound of this woman calling for Alex. His name sounds like a protest. She's so much older than the other mothers at the waterfront. This child was her last chance. She looks neglected – her sunhat faded, her glasses dweeby, her face pinched. Another actress cast to look unlovable. She's

Land (yellow), water (blue), top side of the lilo yellow, underside blue.

Mrs Kintner's terror

searching for her boy but is momentarily blinded, by the light, and then by so much more. Like La Rochefoucauld, she can 'no more look steadily at Death than at the sun'.

4. Disdain
What exactly is Amity, this locus that must be stamped 'Safe'? It is a fictional amalgam of Nantucket, Martha's Vineyard and East Hampton. The kind of place Ralph Lauren likes to shoot his models with their faces

nutmeg-freckled from a day on the yacht. Well-to-do New Yorkers and Bostonians would travel to such an 'elbow of sand: all beach, without a background' and hire a house and put gin on ice and grill the family two-tone (this was, remember, before skin cancer went public and cast a shadow over all the tanned toes).

Except there is a background, of course. Amity would have, not so long ago, less than a hundred and fifty years, been wretched with the business of blubber. Coastal Massachusetts was the centre of the hunt for the sperm whale which provided the oil that anointed our kings and queens, and lit the tapers on our streets. Whales mined from the deep turned into light which obscured the stars! Their skin was lined with a thick fat that could (with no great ease) be peeled from the body and boiled into soupy liquid. Its brain, the largest of any living animal, swilled with gallons of spermaceti, a clear fluid that took to flame in a whiz. Even its intestinal tract, if the whalers were lucky enough to find an animal that was constipated, hid a substance called ambergris, which could be sold by the ounce and used in perfume. The creature was caught and melted at sea and its oil-self sold on land. A strange harvest.

Instead of lilos washed up on Amity's shore, there would have been the swollen bodies of seamen, fallen from whaleboats in noisy moments, unseen and unrescued. A distressed woman at the surf wasn't a rare sight then, before all the whales were killed, and the people had to think of other things to do. Every hotel and flipflop shop run by the defiant islanders – who have come to the schoolhouse this afternoon for a meeting, come to stick up for the glossy beauty of their patch and carp about Mrs Kintner's three-thousand-dollar shark-killer reward – sits where there was once little but one-floor warehouses filled with tubs of stinking leviathan.

But now Amity is deodorised and has found a resource which is sustainable. Nostalgia. One of tourism's first big ideas was the early nineteenth-century notion of the 'picturesque', by which was meant the derelict, the no-longer-functional, that which has ceased to work; the ruined. The link between ruined buildings and ruined women, between tourism and prostitutes has never been hard to make. You tart yourself up and rent yourself out because it's the only thing you've got left to sell. That and Ahab's Amity Fudge. Amity might be a folly but its inhabitants are still watching the sea for signs of a squall, watching the sky for bad weather. A bad season.

There's the requisite disdain in this schoolroom from those who erect a façade for those who accept it. What is this denial of the shark if not contempt for the kid that it ate? Hearing a motelier, the very woman who proudly told Ellen that she could never become an islander, who must have seen Alex's bitten lilo along with everyone else yesterday say 'We don't even know that there is a shark around here!' is like spying a waiter spitting on a steak in a posh restaurant. Larry, the Claudius of Amity, smiling and smiling yet being a villain, is well aware that all the fundraisers

The schoolroom scene

Courteous Quint

and finger buffets he oversees are taking place on the site of bones and toil and widows. Every time the camera finds him in the film he looks like he's hearing an ancestor whispering in his ear *Call this work?*

Spielberg's creation of a crowd is gorgeous. He never dwells, never allows us to remember the names of the characters, but see how many non-characters he manages to have consistently around, cleverly picked-up for another brief shot or line. His camera is low, mobile, close. They're all so plain, these people. The women with their rouge, the men with their chins. Plain and angry. Brody is lost in front of them, forced to watch as they accuse and gossip and complain about the closure of the beaches ('only for twenty-four hours!' soothes Larry). They will not be silent. But the sound of nails pulled down a chalk board soon shuts them up.

At the back of the schoolroom sits a man with a mouth full of biscuit. 'You all know me, know how I earn a living,' he says. They do. Although some of them look at him as though he were a thing of legend, a creature of tar. Quint is a fisherman respected enough to talk with his mouth full. His wintry hand passes what looks like hard-tack to his teeth – a rusk once taken on ships for long journeys, tough as perspex. The actor Robert Shaw elides his words with the occasional chew and makes the islanders an offer. Not three, but ten thousand dollars for the head, the tail, the whole damn thing. If they don't agree, if they play it cheap, they'll be on welfare all winter. He knows the skin and fat of this town, a place on which nature has always played a spendthrift game. Quint has the uninterruptable authority of a man who works. He's a worker in a schoolroom by a blackboard on which he has drawn a shark with its jaws around a stick man. He is the reality instructor.

Watch how Shaw sits and addresses his audience, his legs crossed, his hands very relaxed upon the absolute geography of his body. Watch how he leaves the room with a stare that steals glitter from the light through the window, and a smile so remote, so courteous. In these moments, you can see the great actor Shaw could have seamlessly been, had he been so inclined. Instead he chose another wife, another drink, another book.

5. Control

In walks Ellen. Brody doesn't hear her because he's looking at a picture-book about sharks and can't believe what he's seeing. The mouths on the things. All mouth.

He jumps out of his skin when his wife breathes on him, and she laughs, and then he laughs, and the shock, even though we saw it coming, is a joke on the film itself. It's one of those friendly nods to the audience letting us know our director is conscious of what we're going through together, has registered our anxiety. It's quite the firmest way to build a communal feeling in an audience, to lasso back any straying individual responses. Ellen even takes the book firmly out of Brody's hands and puts it down saying something about his not getting any sleep tonight unless he's careful. Spielberg is daring us to put the book down too. He's saying *Leave, if your legs will carry you!*

It's rare to see such a gracefully self-aware moment of shock. But this is what popular film-making is about. A million decisions about whether the audience has got it, where they are up to, what they're feeling. *Are they ahead of me?* It's about being responsive to an audience like a raconteur, a comedian. I always liked Hitchcock's line about 'playing an audience like an organ'. It's the right instrument for the metaphor. A crowd pleaser is always madly busy – both hands, both feet – always searching for wild polarities of mood and volume to swing between. You can't play an audience like a violin.

Within a minute we soften from this shock into oozily sexy relaxation with Ellen and Brody and their whisky. And then on to broad comedy as, spliced in, two faceless blokes chuck a side of beef into the sea at the edge of a jetty. No ambiguity of feeling is on offer because this kind of montage scene only works through very clearly delineated separate tones: from *this* to *that* to *the other*. You're exhausted, but you know where you are. This is a pillar. That's a post. Beside this, even Hitch can look like a very minor manipulator.

After screening his first movies at the age of fifteen, Spielberg would cycle around the neighbourhood and ask the kids how they felt about what they'd seen. Then he'd go home and play the theme to *Maverick* on the xylophone. This is the behaviour of a fan, not an artist. Not someone into imposing his own standards on his audience, but curious as hell about theirs. *Jaws*, by and large, is film-making by a fan. It is affectionate. It's aimed at perfecting the feelings Spielberg had as a child. Or resurrecting them so that the audience can become like children again. 'I might have become Marty Scorsese,' Spielberg once said, 'but instead the boy scouts cheered and applauded and laughed at what I did, and I really wanted to do that, to please again.' Of course, the danger is that in doing this you'll create and invent nothing. At best you'll simply perfect all the dynamics and stock scenes and situations and gestures you absorbed back then. But the thrill of such a challenge! It couldn't be more modern. And to be able to *remember* that self, exactly, eidetically, as Spielberg does, grants enormous powers.

Spielberg knows we won't leave the cinema (although some reportedly did at early screenings to be sick, but they came back straight away) just as we know Brody can't put the book down. As soon as Ellen's back is turned he's flicking through it, amazed at the parade of viscera, the gnawed torsos, the remains of surfers, gnashers photographed through the silt. They seem to promise: *Now you're going to see something really horrible.*

Back at the jetty something takes the bait. It takes the jetty too. One of the men falls in. When the remains of the platform swing round and start heading back to the shore, towards our floundering man, two pieces of wood stick up as though identifying whatever's beneath as a horned devil. Muted trumpets give a creak like the cellar door in a B-movie. You think *that's not our star – it's a humorous stand-in, a comedy substitute!* And you're right. It's all terribly unthreatening, a joke on our projections, and the dunked slob makes it to shore. The fishermen are just a breather, a fag break, a beat. They push the film up a notch without having squandered anything at all. Like Chaplin, Spielberg thrills to make people want what he feels, and by this point in the film we're in love.

6. Disgrace

At the harbour are high cumulus clouds, and yells.

The first man we see looks like Mr Punch. There are men everywhere, and they all look ridiculous. Men in bandanas. Men with guns. Fat men with blood-filled buckets going out in little speedboats and flinging explosives into the sea. So many shorthands for Vietnam veteran. Even the Labrador panting on the prow of one vessel might be the father of the puppy that would do the same, four years later, on Willard's PBY in *Apocalypse Now*. Same breed, same anomalous suggestion of kindness.

There's so much prating and joke-telling and threat-making going on. Here they are, all the old soldiers still looking for a fight, some of them even trussed up in camouflage jackets as though this shark were prowling through the jungle growling their names, poised to pounce out of the undergrowth. Still, they're not entirely mad. Like the Viet Cong this shark is the *unseen* enemy, and they're in his territory.

Brody shown, as ever, against a window

A terrifying little cameo

So, it's a relief to note a bit of denim, worn low over a pair of boyish sneakers, to note someone moving speedily, but without aggression, to hear a voice, young and satirical. It is Matt Hooper, the shark expert from the Oceanographic Institute, arriving full of sarcy chat.

Hooper talks and reacts quicker than anyone else in *Jaws*, with speedier details, and the actor, Richard Dreyfuss, has kinetic features. Flash-flood grin. Omnivorous cheeks. Hair like some Victorian ornamental doll after a summer lost in the greenhouse. Brody greets him as a brother, his handshake long and exuberant enough to feel like a hug, a gesture so warm, so welcome amidst the farcical recklessness of the harbour crowd.

Brody takes Hooper to the morgue to examine Chrissie's meagre remains. Poor Chrissie. It's her saddest moment. This free spirit trapped in a tray in the corner. The coroner says nothing as he hands Hooper the container, just crosses his arms, makes himself untouchable. He's another of Spielberg's irresistible non-character characters, but with way too much shading to forget. A death-tarnished man who was prepared to support Larry's boating accident claim after some secret deal between them. He looks just like Kissinger.

Hooper's little bad-odour gesture when he uncovers Chrissie is surely unnecessary – she would have been deodorised by formaldehyde days ago. So it's theatrical, symbolic, an ironic counterpoint to the scientific babble he's poised to deliver. He delivers it. Talks about muscles and bones and beasts, some of it in Latin. He removes his glasses and cleans them. Has a drink of water. This is his arena. Where before he appeared to be small, unaccustomed to power, to being listened to, now he's the lecturer, the star.

'This was no boating accident and it wasn't Jack the Ripper. It was a shark.'

Back at the harbour they've caught one. People give exaggerated groans at its stench. A bad smell, after all, is imperceptible to a moviegoer and is the perfect cinematic trope for invisible evil. Except this shark – a tiger shark, Hooper tells its captors as they string it up and examine its bite radius – doesn't look evil. More, a groggy boxer. Where are its teeth? Its

Jimmy Stewart on the dock

mouth is full of as much unhappy drool as that deputy's on the beach next to Chrissie's washed-up remains. It's the first character to suggest a Western.

This animal's been lynched. It's a Jimmy Stewart, punched in the face, blood running from its nose. The arrows sticking out of its head and side make it a martyr. *Arrows*, for God's sake. Some Injuns, these guys, their minds now turning to lunch. Our pity for this dead fish is effortlessly generated. We know immediately it's not the killer, and so does Quint who chugs by, scratching his head and grinning. His boat moves slowly, like an iceberg passing.

Brody, Hooper and Larry Vaughn, a good example of *Jaws'* signature triple composition

Hooper backs into the frame muttering about not wanting to get beaten up. His toying with his doubt that this is the Chrissie killer is beautifully droll. Droll and anxious. You know for sure that Hooper was the plump kid at school who used to tell plump jokes before anyone else did and hurt his feelings. Once he's out of shot Brody's in, and then out, and then Hooper again, all neatly framed inside the curved back of this dead fish. Characters passing plot-batons like sprinters.

The *Gazette* editor wants a photo on the quayside to mark the occasion, proving this animal was the man eater. Hooper wants to cut it open for evidence, to rummage through its digestive tract and see what human remains are hidden there. He's alone in this. The others prefer two dimensions to three. A photograph, which doesn't smell, versus a cut shark which certainly will. Fragrant Amity goes for the photo, recalling the old days as great days, boasting that this community can still farm the sea when required.

Meanwhile, Larry's everywhere, slapping backs. Glad-handing. He makes dishonest physical contact the emblem of this gang, makes them all just bit-players in another bought holiday tableau. Larry won't allow the shark to be cut open. He doesn't want to watch the Kintner boy spill out all over the dock. But Alex does spill out now, in the form of his mother, dressed in shocking black, her veil rebelling in the breeze. She shows no joy at the capture of the shark. She knows who killed Alex.

Death will not be denied: Mrs Kintner turns up, her veil fluttering over the yellow oilskin of the man behind her

Mrs Kintner walks up to Brody and slaps him. Now, a slap in the cinema is sexual. It always means physical attraction, or repulsion-but-there's-sex-there. To be slapped by Mrs Kintner in mourning is like being kissed by a skeleton, it has that disquieting taboo mixed in. But we're so caught up in the film we've forgotten Mrs Kintner too. This slap is for us as well.

The sense of touch in film is so difficult to capture. No punch or stab or screw is real. But this slap is real. This actress actually slaps this actor, and it's the only summoning of touch, of the sense that summons reality, in a film that is – nominally anyway – about being *eaten alive*. (Oh, alright Kingsley, it's simply a film all about 'being bloody scared of being eaten by a bloody big fish'.)

The slap is also one of only two moments of *visible* violence in the film (wait for the other, it's a while away). This makes it a gesture that resonates, breaking the tranced oscillation between comedy and terror which has threatened to become uncontrollable up to this point. And when Mrs Kintner says 'my boy is dead and there's nothing you can do about it' an element is introduced into the film that cannot be resolved, or absolved, by catharsis. This is the extra leap that art makes. To introduce a trouble which cannot be cured by the resolution of the story.

As soon as Brody is slapped, the crowd slopes away. By the time Mrs Kintner leaves, Brody is left with nothing but a dead shark and a plump biologist. Hooper will stick around in Amity not just because this ain't *the* shark, but because he identifies with Brody's weak, bullied cop. If Hooper were to touch Brody now it would be to hand him a pretzel. But he doesn't have any.

7. Love

What does it remind Ellen of, the silence, the cooling dinner, the husband dense with preoccupation? Oh, yeah. New York. Brody, left of frame, is steadily getting drunk this evening when Hooper shows up at the house. No, wait. Rewind.

Brody, left of frame, is drinking. He holds himself as still as he can and tries to think not at all. Not at all. The film breathes very slowly in sympathy. We do not disturb. Sean, right of frame, barely protruding above the dinner table, mirrors his father's slug of scotch with a sip of his milk. Brody clasps his hands under his chin and – look! – so does his son. He unclasps them, trickles his fingers down his face. Not smiling, Sean follows. The exquisite unintrusiveness of a child's sympathy.

Brody sees it, lattices his fingers, unfolds them into a row of Xs, and Sean, realising he's been rumbled, can't conceal his wild grin of joy. Now Brody has the tempo and responds with a monstrous gurn. (The gurn, by the way, and the kid's delighted response, is another of the film's self-portraits, recalling for some of us that orgasm of fearful joy which bubbled up as our fathers, masquerading as monsters and making frequent announcements of the fact, stalked us upstairs to our bedrooms. This is what cinematic horror is: tickling, the primary meaning of which is *You are in safe hands*.)

Sean crinkles his eyes, talons his fingers, and, momentarily, quite forgets his troubles. As Ellen looks on from her bright kitchen domain, Chief Brody leans towards his son and demands a kiss.

'Why?' says Sean, declaratively, which gives us a moment's pause. Brody needs a kiss from his son because he's too ashamed to ask one of his wife. In fact he's told her nothing at all, so her tears of affection as she observes her husband and son also contain sadness at being excluded. And her house isn't the blue-shuttered sandcastle of the first morning. The

Brody's gurn: the love contained within the desire to scare

dining room is sepulchral, the mantelpiece Amish with its pewter jugs and candlesticks. The room has taken too much care over its appearance. It speaks of Ellen's unfillable afternoons, of the Brodys' isolation on Amity. Few parties have been held here. Perhaps none. The new life, you're certain, isn't working out.

'Because I need it,' is Brody's response. A sensational movie line, like something Rick might have said to Ilsa on the runway, but flatly unsentimental at the same time. Children see no harm in being sad. Sean kisses his father where's he's been slapped, on the cheek, healing him, but also reminding his mother of how much she's got to lose.

None of this is remotely sentimental. Sentimentality is defensive. It tries to quarantine a single emotion so that it's uncontaminated by other states of feeling. But the emotion here – love, no question – is not unmixed. It's open to suggestion, and this concise near-silent scene is like a cool hand on your brow. To dispense with dialogue in order to establish character, to find both narrative and poem in silence, marks the young Spielberg. Think of the hero of *Duel* in that diner moments after his latest escape. He orders but cannot eat. He scans faces looking for one harsh enough to be enjoying this terrible day. Again and again you are certain that conference is now required in a film that barely features enough dialogue to cover the back of an envelope. But it's the scene itself that spoke. Of the collapse of the male personality and how superbly unphotogenic it is.

Ellen Brody sees how much she's got to lose

And when Hooper does show up, in a tie, he wants to talk to Brody. 'So would I,' counters Ellen, keeping up a whisper of details to suggest that dust is settling on her character. She's faintly over-eager, like one of Chekhov's spinsters around the new neighbours. Hooper's brought wine – red and white because he didn't know what they'd be serving. 'How nice,' says Ellen, bringing wine glasses to the table. Brody pours himself a pint of red.

It's the only time in the film that something is made of the class difference between Ellen and Brody, a huge deal in Benchley's book, which has Ellen thirsting after the cocktails and tennis of her girlhood and finding sexual solace in Hooper, the academic WASP. Spielberg banned this from the film, because it made Ellen and Hooper vile. Besides, he thought the book was trash. Still, this pint-pouring, and Ellen's punitive little giggle, is a delicate trace-memory of the novel's schematics.

But then, everything is delicate here. It's lovely how much one can extrapolate from the next few moments, while Hooper explains his fixation with sharks and Brody slowly comes round to the idea of taking that closer look at the tiger. Hooper flirts with Ellen, who flirts back, so subtly, almost unaware she's doing so. Ellen doesn't want Brody to leave with Hooper but if he doesn't what will become of them? Brody will become one of the feminised men of Amity. He'll drink more and tell her less and she'll eventually find herself in bed with somebody Hooperish. So Brody must abandon her and go off with his new buddy in order to save them all. He steals Hooper back off her.

It's all expressed through the characters' hands. Spielberg keeps the three pairs in the frame more or less continually, lets them do the real talking. Ellen reaches out with hers, generous but needy, her hostess-reflex coming out of the mothballs. Hooper eats the untouched meal Ellen made for Brody with his, fork moving fast from plate to mouth. Brody picks the foil from the wine bottle's neck, observing. Ellen touches his arm with her thumb, a gesture that both commits herself to him and fends him off. That thumb, gently kneading his forearm – it's all the consolation that can be offered or received. Still Brody picks. But Hooper is finishing the thaw

Sean started, working on Brody: 'Why don't we have another drink and then go down and cut that shark open?'

'Martin? Can you do that?'

Scheider swings his wrist around in front of his face and speaks over the top of his glass, the object that separates Ellen and the house and the hearth from Brody and the new pairing at the table. Actors do particularly like to have their hand-acting complimented as if any fool can pretend with his *face.* But that wrist swivel is the drollest thing I ever saw Scheider do, and the film, on this motion, leaves home comforts behind.

'I can do anything. I'm the Chief of Police.' And just moments before this he asked a question we all want to know the answer to. Is it right that most shark attacks happen in three feet of water, less than ten feet from the beach? What Brody is really asking is *Can we, with our feet on the land, on our own turf, in view of our children and our wives, be taken by a monster?* The answer is yes.

8. Death

There are three kinds of man-eating shark and the tiger is one of them.

It's late when Brody and Hooper go to gut him. He should have been hunting this night, having spent the daylight hours relaxing in deep water. He'd eat just about anything. Cattle. Snakes. An artillery man. All have been found in the stomach of a tiger. Quint once saw one eat a rocking chair. 'We start in the alimentary canal and open up the digestive tract,' says Hooper, cutting. So, in through the surface at last! Into the other side. There he finds a fish and pulls it out like a magician a rabbit. We wait. More fish. Disappointing, but this is the place for realism, for medical accuracy, and the fish are correctly perfect, seemingly straight from the fridge, saved in the camel-like storage stomach of the creature until he's ready for them.

Finally, a Louisiana licence plate and a tin can. Not only does this metal-dinner help us picture the shark as a machine, it also makes us think of those improbable American cars – the width of a pew! The length of a kitchen! – and fancy that this animal has taken one entire, with a beer chaser. What a suggestion. Several times in *Jaws* sharks are referred to as a form of skip, as one of nature's cleaners. The shark as purger of what society could do without, of everything inessential, of the junk of the world. Chrissie the drifter made a perfect meal. But she's not here, only fish and metal.

Brody is drunk enough to join Hooper on a jaunt to look for her killer and on the way Hooper describes the still-free shark as a rogue – abnormally individual, particularly fond of frail humans and their soft flesh. It was a modish theory when Benchley wrote the book, and the film's only now defunct ichthyological detail. All the rest is improbable, but no more than that. Even the images Benchley seems to pluck from fancy, from nightmare – like his Great White treading water, head above the surface, eyeballing his prey – are actually peculiar to that fish. Calling the shark in *Jaws* a rogue sits him with the man-eating lions of Tsavo, who were called The Ghost and The Darkness by locals in 1898 (and in William Goldman's film too). A rogue has personality. He is consciously unruly and ingrate. He knows narcissism. Actually, the concept of the rogue is rather reassuring. He's an aberration rather than the norm. Nature doesn't hate us, only the occasional bad egg.

Brody might be sloshed, but he wears a neat cagoule. This is Ellen's work, you're sure. He couldn't be less masculine than he is now, telling Hooper that he left New York because of the danger to schoolchildren, telling him that in Amity, where there is no crime, one man can make a difference. It's the other way round, surely. If there's no crime then who cares who the man is? Besides, Brody has already made a difference, only the wrong kind. Alex Kintner's blood is on his hands. The speech is a proper nod to the film's occasional variations on the Western. Brody as wannabe sheriff.

They are on Hooper's boat, and it looks like nothing on earth. A spaceship. Hooper represents knowledge in that he can see, with his bank of screens, his sonar, *through* things. His boat gives him complete 360-degree, empirical perception. But the empirical is not necessarily the real. And, anyway, he tells Brody that he bought this boat, bought this floating laboratory because he's rich. What a pair of dilettantes. The gentleman enthusiast and the toy sheriff.

Slowly, they come across the debris of a boat belonging to Amity fisherman Ben Gardner, and Hooper wants to take a look under the hull. The shot of the edge of the ruined craft while he changes is nothing more than a bit of muzak to occupy us as our star zips himself into a new costume. It's melodramatic fluff (that bite taken out of the toast-thin side!) and reminiscent, with its wondrous lighting and smoke, of the fluorescent forest in *E.T.* This is the film's lone clumsy moment. That Hooper, just moments after telling us this monster is a night-feeder and at large in these waters, rushes to get into them is B-flick silly. 'I've just gotta check something out,' he explains, limply. But he must check it out for the subtext of the film to be peeled open. The spaceship, the star-voyage music, the diver's special suit, they promise a trip to *somewhere we should not be.*

Hooper's in. The underside of Gardner's boat is belly-round, ruined by a gash, like the gutted tiger back at the harbour. A triangular tooth is wedged in the shattered timbers. It is the perfect symbol for the creature because a shark is all teeth. It's skin is covered in tiny denticles so vicious it can be used to shape rock. This particular tooth is large. It shines. When Hooper takes it he's Beowulf diving deep to fight Grendel's mother, but finding treasure instead, momentarily heedless that 'death might arrive, dear warrior, to sweep you away'. Hooper covets this tooth, loves it as a relic, can even see it in a display case in the

The spaceship

Smithsonian with his name on it. It's the calling-card the master-criminal has left behind. As Hooper reaches up to take it, a severed head is suddenly staring with its one remaining eye through the hole in the hull. Hooper drops the tooth.

Originally, Spielberg had Hooper shine a flashlight into the hole and find Gardner's corpse trapped there. This didn't raise a scream at early screenings, and so he re-shot in the editor Verna Fields's LA swimming pool, making it ocean-murky with carnation milk and scraps of aluminium foil for silt. Then he jack-in-the-boxed Gardner's remains into Dreyfuss's face, and this lolling head, with its eyebrows raised as if to ask *How could this happen?* is, finally, the dragon guarding the treasure of the tooth.

This is the biggest shock in the film, and of Spielberg's career. Let's leave its position in the All Time Top Twenty to the list-makers. There's nothing technically extraordinary about it except, perhaps, for the length of the set-up, and Gardner being the punchline to those literalist fish inside the tiger. But the film's keynote of above and below is now crystallised. We've seen a wealthy, metropolitan baby-boomer descend from what is presented as a spaceship rather than a boat, through the meniscus, and into the hidden, invisible world where he finds a dead fisherman. Underneath is a repository of reality which is not just separate from, but opposed to, the visible world. Underneath is nothing that can be

The belly of the beast

usefully described in Latin, but the incommunicable. Hell. Death. Things for which the shark is a mere figure.

There are two types of monsters. The first is our incarnation of fear. King Kong, Dracula, Godzilla. The other, of which the first sharkless hour of *Jaws* is a supreme example, is the inflection of the whole of a landscape with fear. Virus horror, the Maryland woods of the Blair Witch, Hanging Rock. In the first type the monster is an irruption of the unnatural into the world. But the second type inverts this. *The unnatural presence is us.* Incarnated monsters usually punish a specific fault. Inflected landscapes make being human the fault. We're the guilty ones and we fear any punishment is justified. Species-guilt is the foundation of modern horror, which means, Mr Hooper, one can forget all about the consoling idea of the rogue.

And what has Hooper, the compulsive talker, whose shark anecdotes back at the Brody's dinner table were so *performed*, so burnished by many tellings, who has twice in this film looked inside the

bodies of things and found only polysyllables, got to say about his trip below? He surfaces into the yellow wash of his boat's lights, and pants and pants and is wordless.

9. Blasphemy

The lilo is yellow. The girl on it is blonde. Maybe she came from that yellow boat you can see behind her, under the sunglassed yellow sun, which is noticeably faded, like a towel after several seasons' duty on the burning sand. An irrecoverable shade of bitter lemon. Once there would have been a wooden cross on the side of the road marking this settlement, declaring it Puritan, staking out a territory for God's elect, huddled as they were between the wild Indians and the huge passions of the great Atlantic. Now there's a giant billboard. 'Amity Island Welcomes You.' Under it Larry and Hooper and Brody squabble. The warring trio occupy a beautifully framed three-minute-long master shot. We see the island for once as an island, rounded by the sea. It looks so bright, so soused in illusory goodness. People busy the background. Visual gossip.

Under this symbol they war. Brody and Hooper are delirious with news and indulge in an exquisite double act, hurling sentences back and forth, as thick as thieves now, telling Larry about this shark and its habits and its tooth which Hooper describes with both hands and words 'as big as a shot glass'. Hooper the bar show-off! 'Wh … Wh … Where is this tooth?' That's Larry, who's presented not as a fool (no burlesque or mugging in this film) but as a politician with an instinct for your weakest spot. No tooth. 'I had an accident,' Hooper grumbles, head hanging. A crude joke made with a gossamer touch to suggest that Hooper befouled himself in the face of Gardner, but it's really more another intimate apology from Spielberg to the audience for scaring them so much.

But this debate is duff. We know Larry is not going to change his mind about the shark. 'I don't think you are familiar with our problems!' The scene is merely a repetition of his earlier *tours de force* of pigheadedness. So Spielberg plays it in a different register. 'I think' – this is Hooper – 'I am familiar with the fact that you're going to ignore this particular problem until it swims up and bites you on the ass!' Hooper's walking backwards, trying to keep in front of the mulishly advancing Mayor, and he brings the camera with him, revealing, as it pans round with a sly straight face the defaced Amity girl wailing HELP SHARK! as a massive black fin bears down on her lilo.

It wouldn't have taken some kid long to paint this. A shark is the easiest animal in the world to depict. All you need is a black triangular

Spielberg the vandal

void, a hole on the surface. It has the most straightforward meaning. Imminent death. And this is what this particular graffito is. A rent in the façade rather than a superimposition, making three dimensions out of the two-dimensional yellows of the billboard. This depthless colour is everywhere in *Jaws*. On sand pails, lollipops, the whinging motelier's polo-neck. And on the oilskin of one of the tiger-shark-catching oafs, dimly visible through Mrs Kintner's black lace veil. It feels fabulously flat and artificial. Fake summer cheer, a travesty of sunlight. And there's no doubt who the 'paint-happy bastard who did this deliberate mutilation of a public service message' is. He is smirking behind the camera.

As the long take progresses, wordily, the suspicion grows that Spielberg is deliberately accentuating the theatrical nature of the sequence. The non-debate, the denial of the town's problem, has its origins, famously, in Ibsen's *An Enemy of the People*, a play about an environmental cover-up on the southern coast of Norway that Arthur Miller once managed to translate with emphasis on 'the McCarthyite forces of mendacious self-interest'. I don't know what the cheerfully apolitical young Spielberg's response was to the Ibsen-lite of early mid-century American theatre, but the composition here (grim faces bandying bad news in close-up against a backdrop which describes the community's dilemma) is reminiscent of the very American concept of civic theatre as upheld on screen in the 1950s by Elia Kazan. He liked to bring his camera around, in films like *A Streetcar Named Desire*, as though it were a pair of energetic eyes in the stalls, greedy for atmosphere and proximity.

Does Spielberg care for the serious Nixonian echoes of his cover-up tale? Nah. This witty vandal is actually parodying the Clifford Odets look – that awful stagy over-earnestness of the political allegory. God, those long speeches filmed from below to emphasise how importantly *universal* everything is! With a polluting tannery in the background.

Here it's just a blonde, a lilo, a boat, a fin. Simple signifiers for the three victims and their murderer. The story so far in official yellow and blasphemous black.

10. Misanthropy

The Fourth starts as light as wickerwork. Bach plays us in. Strings, just like Arthur Hiller used them in the campus scenes in *Love Story* which opened with the line: 'What can you say about a twenty-five-year-old girl who died? That she was beautiful and brilliant? That she loved Mozart and Bach and Beatles and me?' Strings were big in 1970s American cinema, along with mittens and Celtic skin. On the East Coast, mind. Idealising the girl who plays the cello (*Love Story*) or the girl who sings in the choir (*Ordinary People*) or the girl with a faint rash on her neck from her itchy cardie (*Kramer vs. Kramer*) was the sophisticates' response to the hippies. Annie Hall might well smoke grass but she also wears her important tie. These strings in *Jaws* mean plenitude, heterogeneity, people.

They accompany the arrival of the ferry from the mainland, and the ship's shark-like maw disgorges New York in its hundreds. Yarmulkes. Bicycles. Umbrellas. A whole city and its paraphernalia headed for the water. Interspersed among this documentary-like overture are shots of Brody and Hooper frantically preparing for the influx. It's a light parody of the putting-on-a-show, last-minute-panic scene, reiterating the fact that Amity is a stage-set and summer is a stage-managed theatrical production whose date of performance is the Fourth of July. Bathing huts topped with little flags, like medieval jousting pavilions in some silly Technicolor epic are red and white against the perfect sky. But otherwise, the temptation to fill the frame with stars and stripes injecting elephantine significance is resisted. Everything is bright and breezy and sham. Larry has a new jacket and sucks madly on his fake fag. He keeps his hand in his pocket. Not casual. Hiding. He's incensed by all this tense air. Despite the flotilla of shark-spotting boats, 'nobody', he whines at an elderly acquaintance, 'is going in'.

'Please!' Larry coaxes. He's a party host requiring one of his dependables to go and drink the untouched fruit punch. Or more the mad general who needs a volunteer to test a minefield. The old gentleman and his wife link hands with their grandchildren, who are the opposite of loud and bumptious. They are good and little, their haunches dusted with sand, their swimming costumes pink and sweet stripes. The eerie fairground waltz that accompanies them as the four stand up as one is apparently emanating from the Amity bandstand, but it really has no source. It isn't presented as incidental music, although that's precisely what it is. Such a subtle way of not seeming to editorialise. So, they stand. They walk to the waves. Together they go over the top, sacrificing themselves for this Amity, this America, where being cautious and unsmiling and not joining the party isn't just unpatriotic but *uneconomic*. The eerie fairground music is upped. While this vignette belongs to a tradition of the authority-is-mad satire that had been hoovering up easy laughs for a decade by the time of

Going over the top, in more than one sense

Jaws it does so in a murmur. It is swifter, quieter, more universal and far funnier than anything in *M**A*S*H or *Dr Strangelove*. The biggest blessing fate bestowed on Spielberg in the 1970s was an indifference to politics. *Jaws*, like *Duel*, is an intriguing allegory precisely because the young nerd had no agenda.

The dependables are in. Within seconds there's a stampede for the sea. The entire summer tribe make for the surf, forgetful of 'the cloud which has appeared on the horizon of this beautiful resort community' … in the words of a TV journalist reporting to camera on the shore. The man is chipper and slick-handsome. He has tadpole eyebrows. It's Peter Benchley, come to the set for the day and given a speaking role, though he could hardly get the words out for rage over Spielberg's public dismissal of his book.

Benchley had written a screenplay just after producers Zanuck and Brown bought the movie rights, but nobody liked it. What an odd thing. To watch your book sell and sell, to never stop selling, but your script of your book meet nothing but frowns. To watch it being whittled down by Spielberg and John Milius and Carl Gottlieb, and then finally by the actors themselves who spent so much time sitting about waiting for the weather, for the machinery, for *something* to go right, they work-shopped the thing off the page. And then all these non-readers like Spielberg started laying into the actual novel! 'We've made a better movie than *Jaws* is a book,' said the director. Damn right.

If you glance at Benchley's script (www.Jawsscripts.freeyellow.com) or if you've read the novel, you might be struck by their banal dyspepsia. The novel simply conforms to the usual surliness of American crime fiction ('Brody debated rousing Ellen for a quick bit of sex. Just then her mouth fell open and she began to snore. Brody felt himself turn off as quickly as if someone had poured ice water on his loins') but the general tone of nastiness pervades the screenplay too. Quint hacks up a pilot whale for chum in an infernal atmosphere of blood and guts. Sharks eat each other in a hackneyed metaphor for the islanders. One even describes another as a loan-shark. Gah! None of this tone is retained by the film. Thriller-writer and director are both disappointed in humanity.

That's the whingeing motelier on the left, working the party

Benchley all the time and Spielberg fleetingly, for the sly purposes of this scene. But the difference between them is immense. It's the difference between revelling in your bitterness and being proud of your cynicism (Benchley) and not taking it as a personal let-down, not succumbing to hate (Spielberg). It's the difference between thinking of other people as *them* and thinking of them as *us*. The difference between anger and sorrow. Between making things explicit and imposing them on an audience, and making them implicit and giving space for a response. And there are those, piqued perhaps by the optimistic, who praise the former as *dark*, which has become a term of critical approbation. As if sourness meant unflinchingly personal and complex and real. Spielberg's positive temperament is wise rather than bland.

But the whole tone of the film is quickly swerving towards the uncharitable. That motelier, up to her décolletage in water is circulating, a hostess at some excruciating cocktail party. Larry gives a particularly villainous interview to the TV crew, assuring everyone that 'a large predator, which supposedly injured some bathers' has been caught. Besides, 'it's a beautiful day'. It isn't. The weather looks awful. So murky you suspect this comment is a conscious joke, and for a moment the film teeters on the brink of surrealism. 'Amity as you know,' Larry adds, like the chat show guest squeezing in the title of his book, 'means friendship.' In both interviews kids mob the background, grinning, curious, showing how TV creates a sunny surface, demands one even. Film always, *always* sneers at TV and the media. And a surveillance helicopter swoops anxiously overhead. And the shark-watchers are blinded by the surface of the water. And a black fin cruises by.

There's a famous photograph of a public holiday on Coney Island taken in the 1940s, a sepia shot of the land and sea. Only you can see neither. Just human bodies crushed next to each other as though this were the Ganges and the whole of India were in it up to their necks. Looking at this picture doesn't make you think of liberation and openness. It makes you feel crazy. Holidays are when we most hate our own proliferation. There are so many of us! The traffic jams. The swarming ruins. The crawling beauty-spots. Haven't you ever been on a sardined beach and felt the faint disgust that comes when the individual gets blurred, felt something dehumanising in our clamour? It's particularly on the beach where, unclothed, we're less differentiated both from each other and from other species. The crowd is a spectacle. It's easy to feel misanthropic in these moments. A faint whiff of disgust at pullulating humanity comes off so many of the disaster movies of the 1970s. So here, with these babblers in the water.

Below, silence. Nothing but the faint whoosh of liquid passing through the thrusting legs of so many bathers. The seriousness of this

The other side of the meniscus: headless humans, playing in silence

other side, this *beneath*, is an argument so unanswerable that no debate is necessary. See how everyone is treading water, not swimming. They are *playing*. If one thinks of the shark as the efficient ('It's really a miracle of evolution,' said Hooper, 'a perfect machine') and oppose it to us, the superfluous, I think it's a good clue as to why everyone was quite so terrified by the film. Because *Jaws* feels like an indictment of the holiday itself, of the gentle death that sets in over a fortnight on the beach. This, perhaps, is our deepest guilt. Leisure.

The black fin seems graffitied on the screen. Like the one drawn on the Amity girl it has no depth of field – it looks extraordinary because it's so literal-minded, the opposite of abstract. And we can't help but snigger as this big, black figurative fin sneaks up behind a pretty girl and is noticed by bathers who start yelling and heading for the shore. But

Note that the sacrificial family feature, in different locations, in both these shots: not bad continuity but parody

first, they stare straight at it. Straight into the camera. For a few seconds, we are the shark, and you know what? These feeble bathers are fair game.

Suddenly we're aware that Spielberg is making a wonderful joke *against* all the disaster movie clichés he's been toying with. The whole Fourth of July sequence has been criticised as a blemish on the film, as trite and unoriginal. A near-fatal lesion of tension. Surely not. It's a knowingly distancing recapitulation of the Kintner scene, a parody of the disaster movie and a parody of the B-movie. And the purpose of these alienating devices is to crystallise the film's latent but growing misanthropy and transfer it to us. We're actually rooting for the plucky fish now, so all this serves as an inoculation to prevent an outbreak later on. A screaming woman clutches her child as the helicopter flies in a panic overhead. Spielberg holds the shot just a second too long. It's a definite piss-take. A deputy screams: 'Christ! Shark 350! Red 1! Red 1! Do you read?' If Spielberg could have a screwball comedy police siren playing he would. Of course it's all a hoax. Two young boys with a cardboard fin. Just as we were the shark, Spielberg is the boys with the fin, and right now both he and we are under the water giving subaquatic high fives.

'Sh–sh–shark!' screams a girl. Amity's ruined billboard made flesh except in bell-bottom, hip-hugging jeans. And there *is* a shark in the pond, the shallow area reserved for old ladies and babies. It swims slowly. It flies its dorsal fin and tail like the flags of a pirate ship come to sack the town.

Jaws mocks the disaster movie

Or a catwalk model giving us a tour of his statistics. So insolent. It's this *cheek* that keeps these moments from a post-orgasmic fatigue.

'Now what?' says Brody.

'Michael's in the pond,' says Ellen.

And that's right, Brody realises. He sent him there earlier in the day, so he could sail his dinghy in safety, for Chrissakes! And with a sudden ghastly drop in his guts he knows, with the John Williams' theme swaggering into earshot, that this is the real thing.

But it's too late. A man in a rowing boat sculls up towards Michael's dinghy – 'You guys OK?' – and is hit amidship with a broadside from the shark. The rowing boat overturns and the shark's momentum carries it under the keel of the dinghy, capsizing the second boat, spilling Michael and his friends into the water. A cry goes up, and some girls on the nearby strip of sand take notice. They are gorgeous. Their hair a sandy tangle down their necks, their stomachs model-flat. One puts on a pair of specs to get a better look. For a second time the shark turns into beach loser, the ugly guy who has to make a huge and horrible fuss to get noticed by the girls.

Jaws close round the rower and drag him under. And there's Michael, treading water. He is frozen, obedient. A lovely snack. The shark spits out the rower's leg as if it has once more tried and failed to recapture Chrissie, and accelerates towards this boy. Then, with a lovely, sliding camera-motion inexplicably swerves past him. So Michael lives to make it to the sequel in the guise of Dennis Quaid. (Lucky fate. Quaid, so slim in his jeans and rude with his smirk, was for a few months in 1987 the sexiest thing in Hollywood.) Why? That slide is Spielberg the hot-rodder playing chicken with the tragic and the uncommercial. It's where one version of the film ends. Michael, Spielberg seems to be saying, really ought to be dead and I could have told *that* story. But I'm going to make a different film instead. There's a nod to this when Ellen cries over Michael's prone body just seconds after he is dragged from the sea. 'He's dead!' He sure looks it. But Spielberg chooses to duck this, chooses another set of narrative rules, and Michael lives, and Brody looks to the mouth of the harbour, to the sea where it meets the sky. A two-tone blue wall. A desert of water.

*　　*　　*

'Mild shock,' says the nurse at Amity hospital to Ellen. 'Doctor says he can go home in the morning.' But what does home mean any more? Michael will get over this but Ellen isn't sure she will. As the orderly pushes Michael's gurney down the corridor the extra glances twice at the camera as if we've suddenly descended into cheap TV. And that's perfect. In film cliché terms, hospitals *are* reassuring. Sometimes we need ten seconds like this, old staple shots to calm us down. Gentle telly tepidness to soothe.

For the first time in the film, Ellen isn't looking at her husband, isn't fixed on him. He has shunted himself to the side of his own family. Martin is at the left of the frame, Ellen at the right, like a couple sleeping at the far edges of a double bed. Almost unnoticed, an out-of-focus Larry Vaughn wanders through the space between them.

'Want me to take him home?' Brody says, handing Ellen a sleepy Sean.

'Like, to New York?'

There's something very 1970s about divorce. It's when the theme firmly arrived on the page and on the screen. On the telly Nixon covering up, covering up. In front of the telly, parents covering up, covering up. *Pas devant les enfants*. It was never more beautifully understated than right here. Without a cross word, without a heartbreaking cutaway of Ellen tearfully fingering the fridge door art, we understand that the Brodys are finished. No ashtray is hurled, both partners are still in love with each other, but Spielberg has described the dissolution of a marriage. So when Brody says 'No, home here,' Ellen's nod means *It's your last chance*.

And there's Vaughn clinging to the reception desk as if it were wreckage. Then something delightful happens. Brody grabs *him* by the candystriped elbow, frogmarches *him* towards the camera, and makes a little conference room with white hospital curtains. So Larry Vaughn's last scene occurs in the place where we try to keep the lid on death. 'You're going to do what you do best. You're going to sign this voucher and hire Quint to kill the shark.'

'Martin. Martin,' Murray Hamilton says, with his big, watery, liar's eyes. 'My kids were on that beach too.' What the hell does that mean? It's

a great line because, as with all tyrants, Vaughn's last line of defence is the
protection of innocence and the abuse of the propaganda value of
children. *Pas devant les enfants.* Whenever someone's waving children in
your face they're probably hiding something, or trying to bend your soul.
(How quickly the once Hooperish Spielberg came to develop a touch of
Vaughn!) If his kids were on the beach that doesn't make him better, that
makes him worse, and so Larry's gorgeous little *so there* shoulder-
straightening shrug is a gesture which has lost all touch with reality.

Note the priest back at reception leaning around Larry. He's almost
an apparition, a bogeyman reaching to put out a light. Note Murray
Hamilton's shrinking of the mayor – his jacket, his tie, even his hair seem
enormous, as though drifting away from his skeleton. And note that the
pacifier which this big baby has been sucking all summer has finally
flowered into a fag. Spielberg has so enjoyed toying with our craving for a
cigarette. Larry's often-sucked placebo. Dreyfuss snapping in the morgue
'You may not smoke in here!' And that unprofessional quick one which
Brody whipped from his deputy's mouth down at the quay. *Jaws* is the only
film I've seen which acknowledges the cinema smoker's terrible little
internal nicotine spaniel whose ears go up when someone lights one, and
down when they are denied. But one can hardly believe that the mayor of
Amity has quit to improve his tennis. It looks like doctor's orders to me.
And the clear implication of his succumbing is that Vaughn will be back
behind these curtains in a year's time. And not standing up either.

Pulling back the hospital curtain

Brody looks him up and down as if on our behalf. 'Sign it.' Larry can't even hold the piece of paper. He gives an emphysemic wheeze as if the cancer's here already, and writes himself and all the obfuscation and frustration and hugger-mugger out of the film. *This is the very moment* Jaws *turns into an action film.* One can't help mourn the passing of complexity, but you're probably too exhilarated to notice, and probably too exhilarated to have absorbed the beauty of Murray Hamilton's last exchange. Go back and look! The shrug. The drag. The blink. The scribble. The wheeze. His low-level tremor as death's fingers creep into his cavities.

And when Brody whips the hospital curtains fiercely aside they feel like the velvet drapes of a theatre. And the difference between the two acts of the film is right there in that gesture – the denial, the non-incorporation of death versus the absolute refusal to exclude it. You can just glimpse Vaughn over Brody's retreating shoulder. He is standing facing the wall. His stroboscopic jacket at this distance seems bleached white like a shroud. But Brody doesn't look back. He strikes away and strides and the camera—

The Sea

Beneath it all, desire of oblivion runs …

Philip Larkin, 'Wants'

11. Work

—doesn't stop moving until it finds Quint. If Larry Vaughn was the presiding deity of the first half of the film, Quint is the animating spirit of the second. The camera noses around his quayside shack as though off the leash at last, really celebrating the movement from a suspense film to an action movie, concealing the falling away from superior to inferior genre.

Brody is unconcerned by Quint's extravagant scorn, his Croesus-like need for more and more stuff. 'Two hundred dollars a day whether I catch him or not' … after all the man's not greedy … 'Two cases of apricot brandy' … his dreams are just a poor man's dreams of food and drink … 'de foie gras, Iranian caviar and don't forget the colour TV'. Kidder.

It's more Hooper that Brody's worried about. How is he going to get him past Quint when he's gawping about the boat house like a tourist at the best icthyological museum on the East Coast? He's grown fond of Matt but the gleam of scientific enthusiasm in his eyes makes him look seven years' old. On the other hand, look at this place! Although the camera never lets us settle our hands on our hips for a proper stare it's clear the shack is meant as a theatrical abstraction of the sea. Wet and dry. Lobster creels. Ropes and hooks. Mud brown and emerald. The odd lamp from the days of Bligh and Queeg and Claggart, sailors who demanded a complete abandonment of power, who put to sea in other men's souls.

But more it's a shark mausoleum, an ossuary, with fifty, a hundred jaw bones on the walls. It's the precise opposite of Brody's house. Where Brody is surrounded by denial Quint has surrounded himself with what he fears. This is where Quint lives, awake in his nightmares.

'Hey chief, you try this pretty good stuff, I made it myself!' Sweet. It's the undrinkable drink scene beloved of traditional comedy, and

Spielberg's comic inventiveness here is so easy, so natural – no Keystone Cops explosion, no dying pot plant, just a little nod to the set piecelet via Scheider's underplaying as he takes the drink in his mouth and softly stinks it up to his nostrils. Gentle variations on old themes. 'Excuse me chief.' Something's bubbling over on the stove. Shark jawbones. Lunch? Oh, Christ, he doesn't *eat* them, does he?

Delicately, everything is being pushed towards comedy, and it's Robert Shaw doing most of the pushing. Spielberg had wanted Lee Marvin for the part of Quint, but he was snotty about co-starring with a fish. Good. Could you imagine Marvin putting such unguarded humour into his misunderstandings of the boy Hooper?

'I've crewed three transpacs, Mr Quint.'

'Transplants? I'm not talkin' about pleasure-boatin' or day-sailin'. I'm talkin' about workin' for a livin'. I'm talkin' about sharkin'!'

Shaw wasn't as proud as Marvin, although he declared the script 'shit', and he knew about scripts because he'd written several himself, novels too. One of them, *The Man in the Glass Booth*, had been dramatised by Harold Pinter. An obituary in 1978 mistakenly predicted that: 'Time will allow us a comprehensive view over Robert Shaw's career.' But he's still remembered most as a shark killer, and that wouldn't make him grin. 'The Oscars are rubbish,' he once told the *Mail on Sunday*. Don't you believe it. Much of what Shaw said was brattish.

Just before he made *Jaws* he was living in Buckinghamshire with his ten children and needed the money. He was paid more for Quint than any British actor had been for anything. This pleased him enormously. He wanted to tax Hollywood in much the same way that Quint wants Amity to cough up plenty for the bringing in of the shark. Both men wanted their employers to be painfully aware of what they were dealing with.

The hands that Quint seizes from Hooper are 'city hands'. 'You've been counting money all your life.' Hooper messing about on the *Aurora* can bill his fun to the government, and Brody's work deals mostly with parking and jaywalking and kids 'karateing the picket fences'. But Quint – pure work – never lets up mithering at soft, easy modernity. Hooper whips his hands away: 'I don't need this working class hero crap!'

Shaw was born in Lancashire and raised in the Orkneys where his father, a doctor, committed suicide. He spent his teens in Cornwall. You can spot the confusion of accents in his beautifully itinerant voice – his *s*'s hissing like a faulty radiator, his vowels arch and random. Only after RADA and the RSC, in his late thirties, came film. As a young man he'd been too physical to be fashionable, what with this troublemaker's girth, these sloping-back jaws, these eyes the colour of killer jellyfish. Journalists that went to interview him would be forced into a game of ping-pong or squash (he was ferocious at both) during which he'd shout 'I have to live for another thirty years! I have to survive!' Then, in an ecstatic staccato, he would talk and talk about how little he respected film, how he was only doing it for the money, how he was ashamed of his screen work. How he just wanted to write. (Everyone does, of course, except writers, who want to direct.) But self-confessed polymaths are often nervous about their accomplishments. To say you're only doing something for the money gives you the perfect out. If you're never fully imposing yourself on the world you can never be fully exposed to proper criticism.

Shaw could behave like this because he was a natural actor, a glorified amateur. A man's idea of an actor. There's no real menace in this Quint–Hooper battle about male self-justifications, this reality-trumping contest, since it's that most enjoyable of stock scenes – the samurai-search, the gang-casting. And when Quint says 'Maybe I should go alone' it's just Spielberg the flirt, teasing. But there *is* a thrilling subtext here. Dreyfuss the character actor, all details, all devotion to his craft, is under attack from this lazy star, this big tom cat. Hooper and Quint dramatise the tension you always get when a character actor's rhythm clashes with a star's leonine lope. It's about respect or contempt for method. The fidgety versus the high-handed. Understanding versus doing. Which is really work?

Never doubt that the true contest here is between full exposure of the self and self-protection via gadgets, the many bits and pieces of modernity. The film always seems to be reminding us that moderns are children. Here comes Hooper bowling down the jetty with his temperature gauge and his spearguns. His toys. Quint follows with his ropes and his rifle. His bald weaponry. 'What are you,' he asks Hooper, 'some kinda half-assed astronaut? What's this?'

'Anti-shark cage.' Spielberg even chucks in a couple of servants to ferry it out for Hooper, all PhD-ish self-absorption and vegetarians' ponytails.

'Anteye-shark cage?' This always makes me laugh. 'Cage go in the water? You go in the water? Shark's in the water. Our shark.' Yeah, stupid idea. It's Hooper's emblem of detachment, this cage, and Quint has already smashed through it. Behind them, in the Hopperish light sit two children in a beached rowing boat, a little reminder of the simple Huck Finn fun of boats and trips and fishing. Spielberg is bringing everything down out of the neurotic 1970s into a *Boys' Own* adventure story. The film is losing interest in its own IQ, like a schoolkid let off its books.

Then Hooper gives his Hooper laugh. He gave it to the shark-catching bozos when they told him the best restaurant in the island was in the water. He gave it to Vaughn under the Amity girl. And it is truly his director's chuckle. The laugh that the weak give the strong when the strong are blind. The revenge-of-the-nerd laugh. It reminds you that a boy is making this film.

Did people resist Spielberg because he was one of the first *uncool* directors? Not an alpha male, as *director* has come classically to signify – the strong, sexually impressive, socially successful ideal formed by

Hooper's laugh

Huston and Hawks and Visconti, who seemed to direct almost as a reward *for* social dominance. We're so suspicious of the motives of some vice versa person who simply uses his art to make films. Spielberg's rare youthfulness has always counted against him. *He grew up watching TV* was always the charge, which really means *you're unsocial.* Since movies more than other art forms need fresh air from outside the medium because it's so easy to confuse and conflate them with real life. *They grew up watching movies* is the squat complaint often levelled at the post-*Cahiers* generations. It's never levelled at poets. *That Ted Hughes, he just grew up reading poetry.* How nervous Hollywood is unless you've gone out and shot an elephant.

So the farewell to the land is farewell to Lorraine Gary, whose Ellen is the only proper grown-up of the film. That Gary was the wife of Spielberg's mentor and studio boss Sid Sheinberg meant that her casting could never appear entirely disinterested. This only increases one's respect for her performance, given, as it was, over a background of uncharitable muttering. Ellen stands tall in her blue trouser suit and head-scarf. She almost always wears blue and white, fresh and cool, the colours of the sea. Her face is hard and lovely and grave. For Spielberg, adults are women, and those women are capable and never pitiless. And farewell to the best of the camera too, which gives us a leave-taking bow as full of flourishes as any given to the Sun King at Versailles. Spielberg's long shots are untyrannical, as little noticed and necessary as good shoes. Ellen's goodbye to Brody is two minutes' long. A swerving dolly, a focus pulled to close-up, and then the same two things in reverse. Understated. Unmechanistic. Precise, but not seeming so. A yarn-spinner's camera. Story first. The equivalent of long but somehow miraculously uncomplicated sentences.

12. Fun

Come and dissolve into an afternoon's fishing. Companionable and formless. Quint and Brody and Hooper have congealed into the set personae of a comedy trio so likeably you don't notice the film has begun to mark time. To starboard, the boy scientist frowns over some recalcitrant gadget. To port, the hydrophobe in his life jacket and zinc oxide. Centre stage sucking a biscuit the Old Man of the Sea. It's a joke! As you do halfway through telling a good story the film has become conscious of it own enjoyableness and we are calmed. A second dissolve seems to add long summer weeks. Like someone melting into tears days after a catastrophe, the film has taken a long time to unclasp its tension. This long to get over Chrissie.

'One time I caught a sixteen-footer off Montauk. Had to stick two barrels in him. Two to wear him out and bring him up.' Quint's telling a fishing tale, and so now is Spielberg, whose film has this unusual quality of seeming spun, of being made up on the hoof, and always against our projected rhythm. So here's a little languid character comedy Howard Hawks would have been proud of instead of the towering seas of a tinseltown tank. No pretence is made of being undelighted to be off on an adventure. Don't all boys long to go to sea? To escape constraint. Out of womb. Out of the house. Out of the town. Out of the country. Out of time and into a symbolic landscape. From now on in there's only boats and sea and sky and shark. Work! The joy of a task in hand!

It's perfect boating weather. The sea in the blue of health. White tips on the waves and noise hollow on the empty air. This terrific feeling of being stranded – everything ominous and insignificant and narrow and near suggested by this wide plain of water and all that is in it. The *Orca* is

A scientist, a fisherman and a cop

an old and prosaic vessel, the antithesis of Hooper's Kubrickian floating laboratory. When Quint spat about 'pleasure boatin'' to Hooper back in the shack, you now know why. No daytripping marlin-hunter would feel picturesque on this stolid tug, its deck like some cluttered backyard. Brody dollops chum over the sides, and the blood lies on the water like paint on nature.

'Chief,' says Quint, pulling the ring on a beer, 'best drop another chum marker.' Down in one. Crumples the can, famously. Hooper, his beard more Trotskyishly tuggable than ever, counters with coffee and cup. Don't forget, Spielberg was the only one of the movie brats with a sense of humour, and above all, silent humour. Universal, innocent, formal. A real touch of Buster Keaton.

But Brody knows as much about knots as I do. He unties a marker and Hooper's tanks of compressed air come crashing down. 'Goddammit Martin! You mess around with these and they're gonna blow up!' Who could not love this dead scenelet – the planting of the murder weapon. That awful giveaway casualness with which films guiltily insinuate the clue – 'but a small rise in the water level would break the dam and *flood the whole town*. Ah, tea, thank you. Let me show you around the rest of the installation …'

The afternoon drowses on, the wind and sun in our favour. Stillness and sound. Brody's a scout at knot school. 'Little brown eel swims into the hole,' he murmurs, learning. Hooper's a schoolboy with his manuals

The dead scenelet – Hooper and air, his element

perfecting school swot skills. Quint swivels his eye to the tick-tick-tick of his reel. Yes, a definite twitch upon the thread. The big cat begins to drool. Quint, every nerve on tiptoe, pours himself into his harness, like one of those Italian snakes D. H. Lawrence saw as liquid. You don't question this spellbound stealth, even though he's hunting a three-ton fish, not a hair-trigger fawn. Spielberg is trying to stop us breathing. And the very moment that Brody finally ties his knot, smiles a child's smile of accomplishment, forgets who he is and why and where, the shark taps the film on the shoulder and we're off again.

'Get behind me! Hooper, reverse her! He's taking a lot of line.' Quint furiously directs the Chief to cool the now smouldering reel. This film, disguised as a character assassination of an element, is really a love poem to water. Water to disinfect Michael's cut hand in the Brodys' kitchen, water to take the touch of death away from Hooper in the morgue, and now water to help again. A little history of quiet, good works.

But what has Quint hooked? Harry Lime? 'He's gone under, he's gone under the boat! Yes. Too easy. He ain't a smart big fish, he's gone under the boat!' Quint is talking it up like a theatre actor persuading us of something that cannot be lugged to the stage. We are being encouraged to doubt the existence of a special effect. Clever. Quint conversing with a void makes him an actor. When Orson Welles produced *Moby Dick* he played his Captain Ahab as an actor-manager, putting on a show. He understood the deep link between an absence and acting. Bravura.

Quint as Ahab

'Keep her steady now, I've got something very big!' The wellington boot of angling comedy? Hooper speaks for us and says the line your smartarse neighbour is already whispering in your ear: 'It's not a shark. Maybe a marlin, or a stingray. But it's definitely a game-fish.' Snap! The line is bitten through. We've been outflanked by Spielberg again. Just like the guy playing find-the-lady on his Oxford Street crate, or Sugar Ray Leonard prancing unpunchably around Roberto Duran. Always ahead.

And when the piano wire whips out of the water across Brody's forehead, sending him and Hooper hard against weatherbeaten boards, it's merely an imperious swat from the trifled-with shark. He bit through the line. Bored. And although Quint snarls at Hooper's insubordination, he isn't moved until the kid shows himself to be a bad loser. 'Quint, that doesn't prove a damn thing.'

'It proves one thing,' says Quint, with the wistfulness Shaw always grace-notes his tough guys. 'That you wealthy college boys don't have the education enough to admit when you're wrong.'

Pauline Kael wrote that Spielberg 'sets up bare-chested heroism as a joke and scores off it all through the movie'. Right enough. But Quint's macho aggro, his pleasure at rude words, his superstitious songs and explosions, his sad sailor's death, do not add up to the biggest thing in the film outside the shark. To say they do is to cover your eyes and ears. See how Quint's feelings have been hurt by Hooper telling him he can't prove a damn thing. Not piqued but *disappointed* that Hooper misread banter as abuse, that Hooper doesn't understand banter is *helpful*, a system that works. It stops people from running out of things to say. And what could three men on a boat fear more than silence, surrounded as they are by the objectless sea? Without banter hierarchy of power is destabilised and there can be no filial or paternal affection. Without banter this team cannot fall into line.

Still, no real harm done. The schoolboy and the scout are firmly Quint's teenagers, his *Hoop* and *Chiefy*, and he watches out for their cuts and bruises if not their feelings. Hoop flounces up a ladder making faces, to the top bunk for a sulk, it seems. Chiefy now smokes wildly all the time, as though daring Pa to object. His hair even seems longer, fluffed over the ears, protecting him from family blather. Or orders. 'Let Hooper take his turn,' he bleats to Quint, who's up in the crow's nest, shouting down to him to start the chum-line again.

So, Brody is chumming and chuntering and frowning and smoking when the shark at last – *at last* – says hello. It only takes a moment for it to break the surface. Clocks Brody. Gives a tour of his wide jaw. Is gone. What a beautiful gesture, what an Al Jolson wave. Such a cocksure introduction. The opposite of a boneless handshake.

All the things this creature has been! A dirty old man racked with longing. An insatiable psychopath forced to repeat a sin. A scarlet pimpernel leaving a toothy plume. An insolent catwalk model. A Bond adversary salivating at the possibility of an equal opponent. But from this moment he's also simply a species enemy. He now exists as a shark. He exists, and like all monsters, he is *far, far older than us*. And what jerks Brody back, so speedy and rigid it's as if *he* were the special effect, is the shark's silence. Even though its mouth was open there came no growl, no thunder, no list of impossible requests. No proof of this encounter beyond a cool fizz on the water.

Sure you need a bigger boat but there's no time, Brody. No time to crybaby back to port and do the sensible thing. We none of us want to. We want you to get Quint to take a look. Go get Pa! Show him what you've seen. Only then will we really know how much trouble we're in. *Ah, we're in big, wonderful trouble*, say Quint's eyes. Without his uttering a word you

The Al Jolson wave

learn that this animal is Quint's subject creature and his god. Robert Shaw never did very much with his face (it was so very *compact*) but he could act with his eyes as well as Lillian Gish. His irises seem to keep changing their colour as though he'd been made up by a sloppy novelist. At the sight of the shark these eyes take on the tunnel-vision-glaze of the addict about to be satisfied, cramming a thousand-yard stare and a gasp in too. And so his line 'Shut off the engine, Hooper!' (nonsensical, again) is a demand for respect to be shown in the presence of the drug itself, which, for the first time isn't being represented as mere mouth, but an elegant fish.

We know this because John Williams has moved on from swarming gothic strings, past a reprise of the *Jaws* theme, to harps which signify plain amazement. This is his part of the film. Spielberg is now just a Salieri taking down Mozartian dictation. Everything Williams does has a distinct-feeling tone, a definable sensation to it. Martin Amis has said that Spielberg's skill lay in 'beaming down on a specific emotion and then subjecting it to two hours of muscular titillation. *E.T.*, Love. *Close Encounters*, Wonder. And in *Jaws*, Terror.' But *Jaws* ranges so widely and so fluidly through a succession of sensations or keys at this point it seems that the film is actually being cut to the music. Listen to the ignition of the *Orca* whinnying in time and key. Listen to the bleeps of Hooper's tracking device like a figure on the piccolos. And as Quint prepares to fire one of his harpoons which, attached by ropes to yellow air-filled barrels, will bring up even this twenty-five-foot fish, listen to Scheider's 'Now, now!'

The addict's gaze

syncopating the orchestra. The barrel hits the water to a new exhilaration theme, and the shark takes it as though it were a flag and swims and swims and leaves these sailors far behind.

Right before our eyes Spielberg is inventing the almost aggressive purposelessness of his *Indiana Jones* mode. *Jaws* is perhaps the most tonally comprehensive thriller ever made – sheer exhilaration at lacking an agenda or a subject in any classical dramatic sense. The film is sometimes nothing more than a dance to music. Spielberg never meant anything really. But neither did Fred Astaire.

13. Disclosure

We have scotched the snake not killed it. Barely scotched it, in fact. Tomorrow perhaps. It's quiet around the cabin table, the remains of brown dinner on plates. We wait. To a very young child the night is for sleep and mystery, and for the rest of us something not far off. The night's magic is that it's the time when stories are generated, and the place this happens – inside, around fire or food or tables or just each other – is only one step from bed. From dreams.

There are four nights in the film, and they are all idylls of snugness – the opening camp fire, twice at the Brody's toy house, and now this twilight den rocking in the arms of the sea. It's an inexpungeable reflex in Spielberg, who entitled his first full-length film *Firelight*, to return to this time of the day, to save the best for this hour. He never could keep his hands off framing devices which are *this close* to being *and then he woke up!* Think of the sunsetted businessman mulling over the horror of *Duel*. Or Indy tripping down the steps of that back-to-real-life institution. Or the great communal bed in which *Close Encounters'* aliens and human guests are finally tucked up. Even the bookends in *Schindler's List* and *Saving Private Ryan*, the actual survivors and the actual veterans, supposed to relate historical fiction to historical fact for us, are really just Spielberg's coming-to impulse in action again. And we can't help but feel that the *Orca*'s cabin is the place from which the whole story of *Jaws* is being told, like the *Nelly* in Deptford on which Conrad's Marlow spun *Heart of Darkness*.

Quint, like the shark, missing a tooth

Quint breaks the silence that has settled on his lads. Bad for moral, too much thinking. 'Chiefy, don't you worry about that,' he says, meaning a little cut on Brody's forehead. 'It won't be permanent. You want to see something permanent? Ba-ba-boom!' Ba-ba-boom because Shaw, with the kind of grin that sidles up to you and gets you to buy it a drink, is making a charming little uppercut gesture. Out comes his front tooth, explicitly identifying him with the shark. This is Quint the rogue breaking his teeth on the world in his hunger for it.

In every celluloid love affair love blossoms out of a quarrel, and so between Hooper and Quint. 'I got that beat,' says Hooper, surprised to find himself holding a full house. And the scar-trumping contest which follows is as droll and as compact as Hepburn and Tracy trading lines. It's a poker game and a striptease too. Hooper has an old moray eel bite on his arm. But Quint can't extend his because, celebrating his third wife's demise in an arm-wrestling contest, 'a big Chinese fellow he pulled me right over!' Hooper counters in a flash with a leg scraped by a bull shark! But Quint has it covered! A scar from a thresher's tail! Brody, in an isolating black polo-neck, has never looked so lonely. His little improvisation – a glum peek at his appendix – is the improvisation of an actor left out of an improvisation. None of this is mere machismo. One thing you're doing when you show a scar is not pretending to be forever young like the Amity girl. You're admitting that you're moving through time towards death. Gaining stories with the hours you lose. What greater camaraderie can there be than that?

Hooper trumps Quint. 'Mary Ellen Moffit, she broke my heart.' Irony trumps literalism. But literalism is about to conquer. The film switches tone over the course of a laugh from Hooper who believes that the tattoo Quint has had removed from his forearm once read 'Don't tell me! Don't tell me! Mother!' Ah, this laugh. A touch of real art from Dreyfuss that he should be so irritating at the moment we long to root for him. That, given an inch, by Quint he *does* become quite annoying. It's great acting in that it approaches the ambiguities of reality. And technically it's beautiful. This laugh begins with a touch of hysteria and continues into that sort of attention-seeking note that children give. As Quint tells him 'Mr Hooper, that's the USS *Indianapolis*' the laugh hiccups and turns circles and trails. You think this is easy? Try it.

'Japanese submarine slammed two torpedoes into our side, Chief. We was comin' back from the island of Tinian Delady, just delivered the bomb. The Hiroshima bomb. Eleven hundred men went into the water. Vessel went down in twelve minutes. Didn't see the first shark for about half an hour. Tiger. Thirteen-footer. You know, you know that when you're in the water, Chief? You can tell by lookin' from the dorsal to the tail. Well, we didn't know. 'Cause our bomb mission had been so secret, no distress signal had been sent. They didn't even list us overdue for a week. At very first light, Chief, the sharks come cruisin'. So we formed ourselves into tight groups. You know it's … Kinda like ol' squares in battle like a, you see on a calendar, like the battle of Waterloo. And the idea was, the shark swims to the nearest man and then he'd start poundin' and hollerin' and screamin' and sometimes the shark would go away. Sometimes he wouldn't go away. Sometimes, the shark he looks right into you. Right into your eyes. You know the thing about a shark, he's got … lifeless eyes, black eyes like a doll's eyes. When he comes at ya, doesn't seem to be livin'. Until he bites ya and those black eyes roll over white. And then, ah then you hear that terrible high-pitched screamin' and the ocean turns red and spite of all the poundin' and hollerin' they all come and rip you to pieces. Y'know by the end of that first dawn, lost a hundred men! I don't know how many sharks, maybe a thousand. I don't know how many men, they averaged six an hour. On Thursday morning Chief, I bumped into a friend of mine, Herbie Robinson from Cleveland. Baseball player, boatswain's mate. I thought he was asleep, reached over to wake him up. Bobbed up and down in the water, just like a kinda top. Up ended. Well … he'd been bitten in half below the waist. Noon the fifth day, Mr Hooper, a Lockheed Ventura saw us, he swung in low and he saw us. He's a young pilot, a lot younger than Mr Hooper, anyway he saw us and come in low. And three hours later a big fat PBY comes down and starts to pick us up. You know that was the time I was most frightened? Waitin' for my turn. I'll never put on a lifejacket again. So, eleven hundred men went in the water, three hundred and sixteen men came out, the sharks took the rest, June 29th, 1945. Anyway. We delivered the bomb.'

Quint. How readings of *Jaws* love to attack Quint. Our bullyboy patriarch punchbag with two hands on his colossal fishing rod. But how could anyone think this speech is driven by one-upmanship? Not when it clearly inverts Quint from a curmudgeon who has cut himself off to a rogue who would love to come back. All three men on this boat are islands pleading for readmission. Brody wants to be admitted to the community of Amity. Boy Hooper wants to be admitted to the sodality of the grown-ups. And Quint, whose signature shot is the one of him floating past the quay, lonely as an iceberg, is petitioning for readmission to the land, to life. He knows he will never ever get back. This speech is above all a plea.

Quint drinks in the daytime, has no friends, cannot cope with relationships. Even the silent assistant that stoops around after him on land, seen in the schoolhouse and back at the shack, is not so much an employee as that dog a lonely man keeps. Where is everybody? And why does his house have walls made of teeth? The number of jaw bones! It's a repetition-compulsion – never finding the satisfaction he longs for he is compelled to try and try again. Now we realise who Quint's been fishing for. All his lost friends. There is always the implication with sharks or whales, who can consume their prey whole, that we will recover who we've lost when we catch them. This makes them the saddest of animals. If it were lions Quint hunted we could write his obsession off as revenge, but when the belly of the beast may turn out to be merely an oubliette, it's more reunion, or even resurrection, that is promised.

It's only in looking at the speech rather than listening to it that you spot how full of inconsistencies and non sequiturs and illogicalities it is. That thirteen-foot tiger shark, Quint, if you didn't know how to tell how long it was, how did you know it was thirteen feet? If a hundred men were lost by the end of the first dawn, why do you say that you don't know how many men were lost? Because the speech is a collage. Pure impressionism. And it's given its momentum by Shaw's minimalist tonal range – his voice moves scarcely further than the semitone oscillations of the *Jaws* theme itself. Shaw has an up cadence at the end of his sentences which is not a return to the tonic. And this note, this *non-resolving note*, to which Shaw continues to return, sounds like the scratching of an unassuageable itch. He breathes across phrases. He never stops being at least ten per cent funny. The heartbreaking effect is that Quint isn't sure why, or indeed that, he should be relating all this. Behind these phrases is Earnest Hemingway. Understatement. Deliberate repetition. An immediate reigning-back of any emotional eruption. This is from *A Farewell to Arms* 'That was what you did. You died. You did not know what it was about. You never had time to learn. They threw you in and told you the rules and the first time they caught you off base they killed you.' It's the sound of someone's first and fatal disillusionment. The same stifled cry of *Unfair!* that is just discernible in Shaw's reading of the only poetic phrase in the film – 'and they rip you to pieces'.

There's one detail that especially snags Hooper and Brody – Herbie Robinson. Above the surface a sleeping friend. Below, gone. This is the purest articulation of *Jaws*' main theme and they exchange a guilty start of recognition. But the *Indianapolis* story also tells of the obverse of the sunny side. It was never possible for the Eisenhower era to be free of the suspicion that the scarcely believable rewards, all the electric toothbrushes and cars and fridge-freezers and twin ovens, all the mod cons of the baby-boomers, had been parented by the atomic bomb. And so there's a double meaning in Quint's ironic toast, as he raises a mug of something clear and bitter to his shipmates. It is he who delivered the world he so dislikes.

14. Solipsism

Nobody really slept. Quint standing up like a horse probably. Hooper for an hour or so on a sloping banquette. Brody not at all. As the day dawns hungover, adrenaline and booze sit heavy and cold in all three.

The drizzly mist which at first seems to be dug-in clears instantaneously. That's fine by me. The usual line about the weather's incompetently inconsistent performance in *Jaws* is that the film is so compelling we don't notice its patchwork quilt continuity. But Spielberg and Verna Fields wring pathetic fallacies out of the weather so effectively it's as though the inconsistencies are deliberate. When the scenic logic requires sunshine we get sunshine. When it suggests sluggish oily water we get that. When we feel clouds or creamy waves or sunstruck calm that's what we see. Brody bowled down to the beach to look for a missing person one bright Atlantic morning and a minute later found himself under a cloud contemplating Chrissy's remains. And wasn't it lucky for the Amity leader that the weather should so smile on that class-photo-with-tiger-shark moments before Mrs Kintner brought her own cold front with her? There are hell holes on the web full of lost souls chattering about wine glasses which secretly replenish themselves and never-ending cigarettes. The continuity fetishist (always a fanatic or a buff) belongs to a profoundly philistine tradition which can only understand art as the handmaiden of life.

So: so foul and fair a day you don't often see. The clammy weather brings a new tone – fatigue. The shark turns up like a Monday morning. Today is going to be a chess game and White's opening gambit is in chess terms a sacrifice, in movie terms a booby trap. He offers his barrel to his opponents. There it is floating insouciantly at a perfectly tricky distance from the stern of the *Orca*. Hooper gets up on the transom and strains with a boathook – on tenterhooks – to fish it out, falls short once, twice, snags the rope and hauls it in. Still nothing from the shark.

'When he runs you drop that rope or you'll lose your hands,' warns Quint. 'I've seen fingers pulled out at the knuckle! Old seamen's homes full of 'em!' grabbing the coils of rope from Hooper. And when the shark does run he draws blood not from Hooper's city hands but Quint's whose skin we imagined rather like a shark's. Indignantly rough. What an intimate place for the shark to mark, the palm of a hand – and Quint notes it. It's where people make cuts when they want to be blood brothers.

That's it for Brody. He's seen this creature's mouth and he wants home. The boat's engine is shot, ruined by salt water and a headbang from the shark in the middle of the night after Quint told his story and they all sang 'Show me the way to go home, I'm tired and I want to go to bed' and beat their hands on the table and felt for the first time in cahoots. Afterwards they went up on deck and tried to shoot the thing, and, as if in response, there was a shooting star. Which is something we never see in film any more, a real shooting star, a spectacular natural accident. Gone the fleeting image of director and actors grinning and feeling lucky, believing the heavens are on their side. Not when even I could knock up a comet on a laptop.

Well, it's Brody's party, his charter, and it's time to call in the cavalry. What happens next is very droll and very self-aware. For the third time in the film Quint prevents communication with the mainland – previously he's knocked over a flaming lantern to distract Brody from the radio, and lied over the line to Ellen, 'We ain't seen nothing yet!' But only this time are we fully conscious of how deliberate Quint is being. He takes a belay pin and smashes the radio to pieces. And when Brody has his little fit and appeals and shrieks and calls Quint 'certifiable' he looks so much smaller than the man he's accusing. In his black polo-neck he's almost an absence on the screen. Scheider does seem to get smaller in the second half of the film. This is partly a failure of the story and partly a beautiful portrayal of stress. Brody contracts with tension.

Of course he is absolutely in the right. Quint is certifiable. It's a glitch in the plot that Quint has to be seemingly suddenly deeply loony in order to sustain the adventure, but still Quint's response, 'Yeah! Yeah! Yeah!' is the funniest line in the film. Actually simultaneously Quint is *right*. This is fishing. It's a duel, and a code of honour obtains. If you cheat you're a murderer. Our desire not to bring in the coastguard is a winning argument for our instinctive belief in the necessary equity of the hunt. We all of us desire a level playing field. None of us want to feel our heart sinking as the grown-ups are brought in to deal with the monster. None of us want to watch half an hour of the army pointing bazookas.

'Oh boys! He's come back for his noon feeding!' Off we go again. And it's really just a reprise of the first day's hunt only with the many cinematic tropes more distinct, more proud. As the shark circles the boat he's a troop of Red Indians circling a wagon train. As another barrel goes in Williams darts out the kind of jingle you associate with an Errol Flynn movie. Merry and profuse. The men grin in pursuit, their hair in the wind, moving for the moment in pure space. 'Fast fish!' admires Dreyfuss. Perhaps he improvised the line after reading *Moby-Dick*. Brody's not complaining now, is he? Who would.

Two barrels are in! This hunt is so terrifically choreographed and yet it's one of the most difficult-to-follow and inconsistent passages of action imaginable. The barrels are up and then down and then one and then two and then new and then battered and we've no idea what to think. Brody tries shooting the shark again with his pistol. An emblem of the city cop, of his past. The bullets hit but the shark never flinches. Even King Kong didn't like bullets. But then Kong wasn't a monster he was a lover. The definition of a monster in cinema is that it cannot be killed by a bullet. Because it's the weapon that *belongs* to cinema in the same way that a bowl of fruit belongs to painting. And when Hooper whines 'Now what?' it's a lovely moment because by this point the film has earned its right to be free of second-guessing from the audience. Still, we can't help ourselves and imagine the shark is sending a coded message. Do the two barrels mean come and get me? The shark has turned into a real Apache. The surface of the water is just the brow of a hill over which he faces the enemy.

When Hooper and Brody tie the barrels to the stern it's a sign of what a well-oiled team they've become. They lash the kegs and the pressure in the water (and in us) increases as the shark starts eating his way through the line. Most of the dialogue is now overdubbed and so exhilarates things – it's become commentary rather than conversation. No longer an Apache, the shark is becoming an amphibian. How rarely he used to come to the surface. But now, with the sigh of his barrels, he sounds like he has a voice box. His head is out of the water. He is increasing his territory – or rather decreasing the arena of safety for anything else. Marking his patch.

'When we get back, the taxidermy man he gonna have a heart attack when he sees what I brung him!' Quint hits with a third barrel and everything is so jittery, so upped through adventure keys and then smile keys and then horror keys we can only cling to the simple hope that no-one is going to die after all. Three barrels. Symbolically impressive. Like three arrows through an apple or a triple somersault. Or perhaps just three yellow balloons to force this killjoy into the cheerful sunny world. Another gunfight, another outdrawing. When Quint slams a machete into the gunnel, cutting the ropes and freeing the shark, the battle becomes *formal*. The gauntlet has been laid down. How can our guts possibly 'settle on a timetable' (Kael again) with this sort of tone dancing?

The shark goes down again which we've long been told is impossible after the number of barrels and such a chase. Just as Hooper was silenced at the sight of Ben Gardner, and Brody was silenced on the Kintner beach as even Larry was eventually silenced, now Quint is lost for words. He is stupefied. Like the rest of us sixteen years later staring

With this formal, almost oriental, shot the hunt becomes a duel

Damien Hirst, *The Physical Impossibility of Death in the Mind of Someone Living* (1991).
Glass, steel, silicone, shark and 5% formaldehyde solution.
Courtesy Jay Jopling / White Cube (London)

at Damien Hirst's fish in formaldehyde. That astonishing art-work – a poem whose entire text had been erased – was very much the son of Spielberg's shark. It took all the words out of our mouths.

Something happens to Quint there and then. He sets the *Orca*'s

Quint burns up his own boat – his element is fire

course back to land as if acceding to Brody's worries, which is rather difficult to read and a mark of what a long, looping flyline of a performance Shaw has given. Quint deliberately pushes the *Orca*'s overstrained engine. Has he really gone mad? No. It's simply that Quint has found *the* shark which can offer him the chance of a death he can respect and believe in rather than thinking it unjust and cowardly in the Hemingway fashion. *Farewell and adieu to you fair Spanish ladies.*

Quint goes inside and gets changed into a suit for his execution. A clean blue shirt done right up to the top. His old service jacket and cap. He breaks the silence by asking Hooper about the shark cage. Is there any chance it could save them? We could read this as the idiot bully being forced into collaboration by his own failure. But be more accurate. Say that he has his living shipmates, his first since 1945, in mind more than himself. Quint is clearly tired of the miracle of his survival, tired of resenting the fact that he has suffered worse than Herbie Robinson, bitter of the double-bind of having to live happily because of his death. And of having no chance *because* of all that death.

Together they build the cage. Hooper's wet suit is his armour. You think of Charlton Heston being winched onto a horse in *El Cid* as Hooper climbs in. He has no spit to clean his mask. All he dare say is: 'Ok, ok, I'm ready.'

15. Absolution

Underwater drama is an oxymoron. Excepting Johnny Weismuller diving deep to wrestle a crocodile. Recall those ubiquitous quarter hours of a James Bond where 007 is pursued by someone and we're never able to quite guess who is who. Everything slow and indistinct. No discourse. No punches. No opportunity for the combatants to change their minds.

When Hooper descends in his cage the film is attempting to pick itself up from weariness and show this indefatigable shark failing to get tired at a time when we are so tired, so full of dread. On comes the shark, huge. Like an ox, rams the cage with a thud. Surely Hooper doesn't stand a chance! He didn't until Australian documentary makers Valerie and Ron

Underwater combat in
Thunderball (Terrence
Young, Danjaq LLC / Eon
Productions, 1965)

Taylor showed Spielberg their original footage of a great white rubbing himself all over an empty cage like a cart-horse madly scratching his back. Spielberg leapt to include it, which is understandable. And yet this footage of a real shark makes the fiction lose focus. It's the shark's least characteristic moment. The attack cannot seem personal because we know it's no longer a story. Animals can't act.

In only one sense is it frightening. We vault out of a yarn about a shark's animosity towards human beings into proof of the fact. Here's an actual shark looking vicious and unrestrained and filled with ugly things. Out to get us. Still, the shaken and blurred vérité camera giving that authentic feel is just too much pushy camera work trying to inject

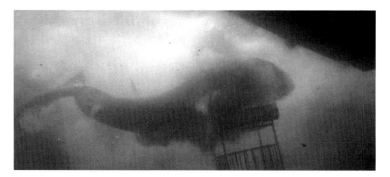

The real shark: you wouldn't want to throw footage as good as this away, but perhaps they should have

excitement into an unexciting scene. It's only because he had no alternative that Spielberg must cut quickly. Everything must be blurred, not through choice but necessity. And the violence must go on and on, flatly, because it has no meaning. Like a psychopathic knife attack.

So Hooper had to escape to make the sequence fit. He strikes ravenously away and down, forgotten by the shark. It's wrong that Hooper doesn't die. In *Jaws* the sea promises a trip to the underworld. Underneath has always been a kind of Hades. Think of Ben Gardner with his wraith's face in his dark cave down where the dead live. Hooper's survival has been cut to fit and muddles something that had been exquisitely implicit. He shouldn't be allowed to hide on the sea floor, safe.

'Bring her up!' goes the shout. As the battered cage is hauled to the surface the crane smashes against the gunwale of the boat nearly decapitating Brody. Things are falling apart. When the *Orca* lists right over, junk collects down the bottom end as in some significant West End play imagining the world out of joint. On the soundtrack now, an almost imperceptible high-pitched hum. The sound of pure hatred. Or precognition. The stir of an incredibly alert human being. It seems to belong to Quint, or to be heard only by him. This man so attuned to his fate. The shark seems to coalesce out of this sound, leaping onto the transom, its body almost fully exposed, as though trying to be born.

'Nobody knows how long they live. A thousand years, maybe two,' said Brody to Ellen after looking at his picture book. Sharks were ancient when the dinosaurs walked the earth and they haven't altered, not a jot. But how long a single Great White can live is hard to say. Perhaps as long as a turtle. Not one has been tagged or held captive long enough to find out. Like that other prehistoric fish, the coelacanth, confinement spells ruin. So it isn't impossible that this is the same shark that fed on Herbie Robinson. It's a clear possibility.

He is scarce, fond of his own company, swimming with the short, stiff tail strokes of any swift, deep-sea fish. His triangular teeth, precisely the same shape as his dorsal fin, are arranged in rows, always some lying flat in wait like fallen dominoes. He saws and then swallows directly for these teeth are not meant to chew. Month-old limbs have been found in his stomach with the wedding rings still on the fingers, the very thing that shone pale and first caught his eye. His twenty-five feet make him bigger than most but not impossibly so. Bites on whale carcasses tell of larger Great Whites far from the shore, far from surfers and swimmers and their soft flesh. How vain we are to think that they like to eat us because we are sweet! It is because we are slow and easy like an old seal that they attack. And they rarely do.

He can rush into the air entire to snatch a seabird. He can live almost anywhere in the world, in the Gulf of Alaska and the Mediterranean, off the coasts of Africa and southern Chile. A nudge from him can ram an object with a force equivalent to a ten-pound weight dropped from a height of fifty feet. So boats have never frightened him much. In 1595 one took a sailor who was 'hung downe with halfe his body into the water to place our rudder upon the hookes, and there it came and bit one of his legs to the middle of the thigh, cleane off at one bite, notwithstanding that the Master stroke at him with an oare …'

And on the *Orca* he shows his mouth, so deep. Everything that the sea has both concealed and represented. The silencer. The subtext. The shied-from reality. How the world loves to gaze at this maw. How editors rely on it for supplement covers knowing it's as irresistible a draw as a sad

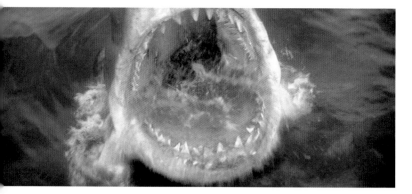

The shark's maw, one of the most irresistible images of death

Monroe. Why? Because it is the clearest signifier of death there is. We can be bitten by a spider. Stung by a jellyfish. Mauled by a bear. Gored by a bull. Constricted by a python. Trampled by an elephant. *Eaten* by a shark. Only through the shark's jaws is the other side visible – the actual place where the victim will be moving to. It is a topological description of the after-life. You can be swallowed by a whale and still live. But the shark's jaws are the physical gates to the next world. A portal at which you stare and stare trying to discern the other side of life. It's the one thing that asks you to puzzle it out, compelling a question to which you will never living know the answer.

Now, Spielberg and his generation grew up frustrated in front of chunky stunt men in rubber suits pretending to be a creature from a lagoon. Or iguanas stumbling over trees made from matchsticks. The monstrous, unmonstery letdown of the unrealistic beast! The revelation of the creature was always a fiasco of bathos. How strong the longing to see a monster and believe the bloody thing. The longing to sate the pornographic desire to see what is being fudged. The longing to trust in a chimera come from the optical illusion of twenty-four frames per second.

Spielberg's greatest interest when he was a kid was special effects. He made myriad explosions from flour, vomit from bread. And so for him this shot of this shark is the moment of truth. He wants to work magic. He

The shark exposed and nearly, but not quite, bathetic

wants to make us see, even if in so doing we leave the world of make-believe and join the world of believe. And when you do get to look into this thing, into this mouth, your literal-mindedness catches up with you as the image slowly drifts back the harder you stare, from three dimensions back to two. You know you're staring at a bit of black pigment or a bit of pink pigment. But it's not even relevant that this creation of fiction, this story made real, looks rubber (although actual Great Whites hardly look likely – they have *gums* for god's sake, their snouts wrinkle as they poise to bite, their gullet expands like a pelican's). We have believed enough in *Jaws* that no phoney gill could ruin it for us now. Richard Attenborough's obsession – 'I just wanted to make people see' – in *Jurassic Park* is actually a confession of the film's utter failure. Spielberg had by then with his computers finally made us see all over the place, almost every moment, the story crammed in between a trumpeted T-Rex. Finally, he had made credibility no longer an issue in the world of beasts. And what a waste of his talent. What a fool's errand, tagging along after reality. Because the pursuit of reality has nothing to do with art. So, we finally got to see and all we could say was, well done! One of the enemies of fiction is our growing capability to see through it.

This rubber shark has a reality far in excess of, say, the computer-generated sharks of *Deep Blue Sea*. In *Jaws* the event is actually enacted and an action surely must be undergone for it have any reality. Here there really is a simulacrum of a shark heaving onto a transom, half sinking a ship beneath him, straining and straining to reach Quint. And Shaw is not lying on some blue screen imagining how teeth might feel if they closed around his ribs. The actor and the machine were there, one day in 1975, acting out 'Death by Shark', no matter if those closing teeth are false. It is vital for fiction to be vulnerable, to be puncturable by moments of disbelief, because all fiction is dressing up, make-believe, playing about. Kids' stuff. But fiction saves its greatest rewards for any act of faith in a witness.

Spielberg also grew up *enjoying* his laughter at the rubber men and iguanas, and retained a touch of cynical coarseness, a lack of faith in the magic, in a giggling geeky, male-bonding sort of way. That was the

Steven Spielberg and shark, on the set of *Jaws*

Spielberg that wanted to sell Jawberry and Sharklet ice-cream at screenings and called the shark 'Bruce' after his lawyer and suggested the film end with a thousand fins heading towards Amity. The guy with no illusions. This is why the film is never too solemn, always held open to those who would laugh their way through it. But at the same time it never gives you a clear direction to laugh. And when the shark leaps on board the fantastic tension between these two forces – the faithful and the sniggering – is about to have its final battle.

Quint drops closer towards the waiting teeth, a bandanna tied around his head like a kamikaze pilot. He pants in panic. This is not a sound you expect from this man, a pant. His eyes are now a dim green. As the boat heaves more and more vertical we pray he might drop into death's belly without once being bitten. The deck of the boat is now a table serving Quint to the shark. Quint reaches up to Brody who grabs his

The hands motif finally pays off

gloved hand – the very one marked by the shark. Hands. Three times in the film handshakes connect land and the sea. Ben Gardner welcomed Hooper out of a boat onto Amity. Then there were the night fishers helping each other out of the water. But Quint has a glove on his hand because he's not connected to any community. He doesn't come from fiction, he comes from fact. The *Indianapolis*. And it would be a fracturing of the rules of fiction to rehabilitate Quint because his story doesn't belong to the film but history.

There is only one death in the film which is visible and this is it. Only one shark bite as it were. And when the shark bites Quint the hot

Quint meets his destiny

The shark crashes through the *Orca*'s cabin window

sorrow is appalling. Blood comes up through his teeth in its bright familiar colour. No-one happening on this scene, this second or two, could imagine what had caused such a colour. This is the other great bathetic moment in fiction. Death. It's the greatest moment of make-believe, demanding we turn a blind eye to swords in armpits and hidden blood packs. With Quint's death we have both the thing you can't look at directly (death) and thing you can't take your eyes away from (the maw). And it's the most vulnerable and daring moment with its long, undisguised takes and no music showing us a frank unsmiling thing. It's the most difficult shot in the film and you feel your own

The minute hand ticks

belief stretched but never breaking. It plays right on the edge of credibility; it just might push us too far and collapse like a soufflé. How tonally complicated – trying a magician's flourish, daring to play with the possibility of humour, and yet *not* be laughed at. The many people who have chuckled at Quint's death and think it's a moment of high comedy are making a self-congratulatory over-simplification. I don't believe them.

Just Brody left now. The shark comes through the window of the almost fully submerged *Orca* after him. Brody feeds him an oxygen tank. Still no music. Breathing and water. He is going to die. You hate the shark for Quint. You feel he's already got what he wanted and so he deserves to lose because in coming back for more he is greedy. Over-confident.

The boat is almost gone. Chiefy's land has diminished from a city to an island to a boat to the top of a mast. Soon all there will be left is the surface of the sea, as if the monster has consumed the film itself. Brody clambers up the mast with Quint's rifle. The man-of-action's rifle which he must combine with the man of science's air tank to kill this shark. Quint with his oil lamp and his rifle and his smoking boat is fire. Hooper the 'half-assed astronaut' with his waffle and his oxygen tanks is air. Brody earth. If the shark wins, the land will be its territory, and so one of them has to swap over.

So here we are on the cross-trees with the mast ticking like a minute hand towards the horizontal. The shark is headed for Brody so the moment the lateral motion of this minute hand will touch on the ocean is the moment he will die. Music. It's going to be ok! Spielberg (naturally) decides on a final gunfight and as the shark comes at Brody and his rifle he is Clint – the great silent character of modern film, the man with no name – chewing on a cheroot.

Spielberg's sense of emotional timing is pristine. We don't need any more tension, and the music is there to build us up to our catharsis. Brody misses, misses again, misses one more time. 'Smile you sonofabitch!' he shouts, pulling the trigger, firing the bullet, hitting the air tank, exploding the shark. Smile you sonofabitch. The shark has been *the* figure lacking in humour in what is basically a film that tries to

Echoing the iconography of the Western: Clint Eastwood in *Per Qualche Dollaro in Più / For a Few Dollars More* (Sergio Leone, PEA / Arturo Gonzales PC / Constantin Film AG, 1965)

be cheerful. Brody's words make explicit the film's fight between comedy and tragedy. It's as if Spielberg's whole sunny world is menaced by the unsmiling. It's also the first time anyone's really insulted the shark, and at its first insult the bully is blown up. The other thing being exploded is all that rather masculine, foolish desire to bring back and demonstrate some palpable embodiment of the impalpable. No-one else will see this shark, and when Brody says *It was this big* no-one will quite believe him. Before Quint saw the shark for what it was he wanted to bring it home to the taxidermy man, and Hooper was so disappointed to have lost his tooth. So Brody blows up the boastfulness of the hunter and purifies the action of killing.

The final images

Joy! Land and air and water and fire combine in this success so huge and farcical. The final action of the film is to make you *delighted*. Look at the joy on Scheider's face! You don't often get that in a thriller. And Scheider is dunked when he blows the creature up. He is baptised. The action of going under is his bow to a worthy opponent. Hooper comes to the surface rather sheepishly as though he knows he ought not to be alive. He finds Brody and asks after Quint. 'No,' says Brody. They had been friends, you know. But these two are glad to be alive and when they laugh together it's a laugh which acknowledges luck, which comprehends rather than runs away from death. They kick for home using the yellow barrels of air to support them. Spielberg seems to be saying that the sunshine side can sustain you if you proceed with the knowledge that it's a necessity for keeping us afloat rather than a screen painted over what we would deny.

The film returns our pulse rate to normal with such modest credits. Just like an actual roller coaster does, quelling its pace, gliding you back to a stop at your starting-point. The beach. We step off this film so gently just as in the distance Brody and Hooper step out of the tide. The curve of the shoreline seems to embrace the ocean as if land and sea are friends again. Brody is now a figure in a panorama from which he will never again feel separated. Just before the screen goes black I strain to see him. But like Sylvia Plath in 'Daddy' can only see the Atlantic – 'Where it pours bean green over blue, in the waters off beautiful Nauset.'

Credits

JAWS

USA
1975

Directed by
Steven Spielberg
Produced by
Richard D. Zanuck,
David Brown
Screenplay by
Peter Benchley,
Carl Gottlieb
Based upon the novel by
Peter Benchley
Director of Photography
Bill Butler
Film Editor
Verna Fields
Production Designer
Joseph Alves Jr
Music by
John Williams

© Universal Pictures

Production Company
a Zanuck/Brown production
Production Executive
William S. Gilmore Jr
Unit Production Manager
Jim Fargo
Production Assistants
Barbara Nevin, Richard
Fields
First Assistant Director
Tom Joyner
**Second Assistant
Director**
Barbara Bass
Script Supervisor
Charlsie Bryant
Location Casting
Shari Rhodes
Casting Assistant
Janice Hull
Script Collaborators
Howard Sackler,
John Milius, Robert Shaw
**Live Shark Footage
Filmed by**
Ron Taylor, Valerie Taylor
Underwater Photography
Rexford Metz
Camera Operator
Michael Chapman
Camera Assistant
James A. Contner
Stills
Louis Goldman
Special Effects
Robert A. Mattey

Set Decorations
John M. Dwyer
Quint's Boat Design
Peter Eldridge
Costumes
Irvin W. Rose
Cosmetics by
Cinematique
Make-up
Del Armstrong
Titles & Optical Effects
Universal Title
Sound
John R. Carter, Robert Hoyt
Sound Editor
Jim Troutman
Technical Adviser
Manfred Zendar
Shark Expert
Peter Gimbel
Transportation
Charlie Blair
Stunt Co-ordinator
Ted Grossman
Stunt Performers
Carl S. Rizzo,
Richard Warlock
**The Producers Gratefully
Acknowledge the
Co-operation of**
The National Geographic
Society and
Mr L. J. V. Compagno of the
Department of Biological
Sciences, Stanford
University

Cast
Roy Scheider
Chief Martin Brody
Robert Shaw
Captain Quint
Richard Dreyfuss
Matt Hooper
Lorraine Gary
Ellen Brody
Murray Hamilton
Mayor Larry Vaughn
Carl Gottlieb
Ben Meadows, the editor
Jeffrey C. Kramer
Lenny Hendricks
Susan Backlinie
Christine 'Chrissie' Watkins,
first victim
Jonathan Filley
Tom Cassidy
Ted Grossman
estuary victim
Chris Rebello
Michael Brody
Jay Mello
Sean Brody
Lee Fierro
Mrs Kintner
Jeffrey Voorhees
Alex Kintner
Craig Kingsbury
Ben Gardner
Dr Robert Nevin
medical examiner
Peter Benchley
TV interviewer

[uncredited]
Ed Chalmers
Bob Chalmers
fishermen attacked by shark
Al Wilde
Keisel
Hershel West
Quint's mate
Dwight Francis
old man at beach
Frank Murray
kiosk owner
Woodrow Wilson Sayre
John Alley
Stan Hart
John Painter
Bill O'Gorman
Donald Poole
Fanny Blair
Eleanor Harvey
William Blood
Henry Carriero
Carol Feiner
Arthur Young
Stephen Carey Luce
Carol Fligor
Maggie Moffett
William Abbe
Arthur Nicol
Crosby Foster
George Silva
Tom Joyner
Andy Stone
people on the island

Colour by
Technicolor
2.35:1 [Panavision]

11, 221 feet
125 minutes

**Made at Martha's
Vineyard,
Massachusetts/Australia**
MPAA: 24175

Credits compiled by
Markku Salmi, BFI
Filmographic Unit

Note on Sources

When I first started thinking about writing a book on *Jaws*, I popped out to the shops and quickly discovered that someone else had written it. *Jaws* by Nigel Andrews (London: Bloomsbury, 1999) is just perfect, the opposite of stiff, a clutch of shark stats, production details, autobiography, marketing gossip and a long interview with Roy Scheider. My copy of it has now fallen apart, and I'm scrambling to get hold of another. (Bloomsbury have stopped publishing their Pocket Movie Guides for some reason, they were cigarette-packet-sized and so convivial.) I mentioned in the introduction that Carl Gottlieb's *The Jaws Log* (London: Faber and Faber, 1975), apparently a modest little amble, is the sharpest 'making of' book in circulation, distinct from classics like Lilian Ross's *Picture* (about *The Red Badge of Courage*) and Julie Salomon's *The Devil's Candy* (about *Bonfire of the Vanities*) in that it's written by a member of the production, and uncontaminated by handwringing. Spielberg hated it, since it details how collaborative an effort *Jaws* was (a fraught subject – the tussle over who wrote precisely what part of the script goes on.) It is excellent on producers Zanuck and Brown, on Universal, on how Murray Hamilton was sprayed by a skunk outside his hotel one drunken night. You name it. It's a rapacious read, and contains some great photos too – one shows Shaw and the shark seemingly snoozing on the ruined afterdeck of the *Orca* between takes. They look like pals.

    Close to the Shore by Michael Capuzzo (London: Headline, 2001) is an account of the killings off the Jersey Shore in 1916 that provided the model for Peter Benchley's novel *Jaws* (Garden City, NY: Doubleday, 1974). At the turn of the century experts believed sharks hadn't the jaw strength to hurt a man, and Capuzzo's use of clippings from the *Baltimore Sun*, the *Matawan Journal* and the *Fishery Bulletin* give a clear record of public perception changing and exploding. There's lots of thrilling shark information in here too. *In the Heart of the Sea* (London: HarperCollins, 2000) by Nathaniel Philbrick tells of the sinking of the whaleship *Essex* by a spermwhale in 1820 – the story behind *Moby-Dick*. This is a great book for anyone wanting to know more about the Nantucket whalers, their ordeals, their community. Then again, you could just read Melville. *Great Shark Writings*, edited by Ron and Valerie Taylor (Woodstock, NY: Overlook Press, 2000), who shot the live shark footage for *Jaws*, is simply a volume containing a selection of literature on sharks. There's Hemingway in here and Arthur C. Clarke, but most of these chapters are pretty prosaic accounts of shark bites and feeding habits. Nevertheless it's a very solid reference book for anyone wanting shark facts and figures and gasp-making details. Each excerpt is introduced – and sometimes put firmly in its place – by the protective Taylors.

Shark: A Photographer's Story by Jeremy Stafford-Deitsch (San Francisco, CA: Sierra Club Books, 1987) contains the best photographs of the Great White I've come across. What do they really look like? Rubbery and unrealistic. I found the *Steven Spielberg Interviews* edited by Lester D. Friedman and Brent Notbohm (Jackson: Mississippi University Press 2000) particularly handy. It contains interviews with Spielberg from as early as 1974, catching him being very dweeby about working with Joan Crawford on the TV show *Night Gallery* and then, moments later, crystal clear about Benchley's novel and the problems he had with its plotting and grubby characters. This interview took place during filming and Spielberg is not yet pooped by the whole experience – is raring to go. It's possibly the only interview with him about *Jaws* that isn't suffused with a kind of annoyance. Joseph McBride's *Steven Spielberg: A Biography* (London: Faber and Faber, 1997) is detailed, methodical, well-nigh definitive, very strong on the director's childhood and utterly defeated by its dead-bat protagonist. Spielberg simply refuses to be interesting. In common with much Spielberg literature, McBride's biography sort of has to overrate *ET* and *Schindler's List* in order to sustain the narrative. Saying you preferred the early stuff tends to muck up the shape of your book. *Steven Spielberg: The Post-Duel Decline* is just something I made up.

The Oxford Book of the Sea edited by Jonathan Raban (Oxford: Oxford University Press, 1991) is a brilliant anthology of writing about the sea from *The Book of Common Prayer* to John Updike in *Rabbit at Rest* describing the twinkle of bathing suits as a 'long gray string vibrating along the bay for miles …' I used this book all the time, for all sorts of reasons, not least the way in which it led me to view sea writing in new ways, to understand, along with Henry Kisor 'the currents that bind it, and the promontories that divide it'.

Also Published

L'Argent
Kent Jones (1999)

Blade Runner
Scott Bukatman (1997)

Blue Velvet
Michael Atkinson (1997)

Caravaggio
Leo Bersani & Ulysse Dutoit
(1999)

Crash
Iain Sinclair (1999)

The Crying Game
Jane Giles (1997)

Dead Man
Jonathan Rosenbaum
(2000)

Don't Look Now
Mark Sanderson (1996)

Do the Right Thing
Ed Guerrero (2001)

Easy Rider
Lee Hill (1996)

The Exorcist
Mark Kermode (1997,
2nd edn 1998)

Eyes Wide Shut
Michel Chion (2002)

Independence Day
Michael Rogin (1998)

Last Tango in Paris
David Thompson (1998)

**Once Upon a Time in
America**
Adrian Martin (1998)

Pulp Fiction
Dana Polan (2000)

The Right Stuff
Tom Charity (1997)

**Saló or The 120 Days of
Sodom**
Gary Indiana (2000)

Seven
Richard Dyer (1999)

The Silence of the Lambs
Yvonne Tasker (2002)

The Terminator
Sean French (1996)

Thelma & Louise
Marita Sturken (2000)

The Thing
Anne Billson (1997)

**The 'Three Colours'
Trilogy**
Geoff Andrew (1998)

The Usual Suspects
Ernest Larsen (2002)

Titanic
David M. Lubin (1999)

Trainspotting
Murray Smith (2002)

The Wings of the Dove
Robin Wood (1999)

**Women on the Verge of a
Nervous Breakdown**
Peter William Evans (1996)

**WR – Mysteries of the
Organism**
Raymond Durgnat (1999)